All I Ever Needed to Know I Learned From My Golf-Playing Cats.

D1280701

a collection of

TOM the DANCING BUG

comic strips

BY RUBEN BOLLING

NANTIER · BEALL · MINOUSTCHINE
Publishing inc.
new york

This book has nothing whatsoever to do with the heartwarming sentiment that

All I Ever Needed to Know I Learned From My Golf-Playing Cats.

It does not include such whimsical notions as:

Purr together,
Putt together.
RRRRR
RRRRR
17.

Don't get distracted when you're going after a birdie.
28.

The wise feline makes the most of a sand-trap lie.
KICK KICK
34.

And the following nonexistent publications never said the following about it:

"If you love cats and golf and trite inspirational messages, then you probably buy a ton of crappy gift books. Why not add this one to the pile?"
-*The Crappy Gift Book Enthusiast*

"This surefire title pushes all the book-buying buttons! I bought three immediately. I would have bought another if it had some reference to how men and women are different. Or if the author was anonymous!"
-*Book Titles Magazine*

"If you read just one book the next time you visit the bathroom, let it be this one!"
-*The Lavatory Librarian*

TOM the DANCING BUG

©1993 RUBEN BOLLING

DIST. BY QUATERNARY FEATURES · P.O. BOX 72 · N.Y., N.Y. · 10021

SHLUFF
IT SLEEPS AMONG US!

FROM THE GREAT VASTNESS OF SPACE, IT CAME TO EARTH!

I AM SHLUFF, FROM THE PLANET DORMARR!

Eat at Nick's

I AM HERE TO TAKE A NAP ON YOUR PUNY PLANET! DO NOT TRY TO STOP ME!

AND SO DID THE BEHEMOTH SETTLE ITS MASSIVE BODY AND COMMENCE TO SLUMBER!

ZZZz

OUR WORLD'S GREATEST SCIENTISTS LABORED TIRELESSLY TO FIND A WAY TO RID THE EARTH OF SHLUFF!

HOW LONG WILL IT SLEEP?

WE KNOW NOT! A NAP TO THIS GIANT ALIEN COULD LAST CENTURIES!

BUT AFTER TWO AND AND A HALF HOURS DID SHLUFF WAKE UP AND LEAVE THIS WORLD, AS MYSTERIOUSLY AS IT CAME!

IT WAS A GOOD NAP!

THE END...?

ENDANGERED SPECIES

TOM the Dancing Bug

AND THEIR PRESS AGENTS

©1993 ruben bolling

SNOW OWL

LISTEN, BABE, I'M NOT BRAGGING, BUT I **INVENTED** THIS WHOLE FEKAKTA BUSINESS! AFTER I PUT THESE BIRDS ON THE MAP, EVERY SPECIES REALIZED THAT THE NAME OF THE GAME IS **PUBLICITY!**

HERB KRAMER

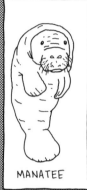

MANATEE

SO I SAID, "I SEE THE COVER OF 'TIME'! I SEE THE 'DISCOVER CHANNEL'! BUT **COME ON! MOVE** A LITTLE! JUMP THROUGH HOOPS! **PEP** UP, FOR GOD'S SAKE!"

BARB PECOTA

TIGER SHARK

OKAY, SO WE'VE GOT THE "MONSTER OF THE DEEP" THING WORKING AGAINST US. BUT IF WE PLAY UP THE MYSTERIES OF SHARKS' IMMUNOLOGICAL SYSTEMS, PLUS THE FRAGILE MARINE ECOSYSTEM, WE'LL GET EXPOSURE OUT THE WAZOO!

SAMUEL DOUGLAS

AMAZONIAN TWIG NEWT

I FIGURE OUR BEST BET IS JUST TO LATCH ON TO THE WHOLE RAIN FOREST DEAL. I MEAN, IT'S NOT LIKE I'M GONNA GET A STORY ON "60 MINUTES"! IT'S JUST ANOTHER FRIGGIN' LIZARD!

JAMES HACKETT

BLACK-BELLIED NEW GUINEAN DUNG BEETLE

HEY, MY CLIENT ISN'T EXACTLY A KOALA BEAR. BUT I'M STARTING OUT IN THIS BUSINESS. I'M IN TOUCH WITH THE PEOPLE HANDLING THE **BROWN-BELLIED** NEW GUINEAN DUNG BEETLE. WE MIGHT WORK TOGETHER.

LAUREN RIBERIO

BACTERIA FL7-138A

ALRIGHT, I'M NOT SAYING WE DON'T HAVE AN UPHILL BATTLE. BUT I'M MAKING A LOT OF CALLS. I THINK A GUY AT THE "QUARTERLY JOURNAL OF BACTERIUM AND VIRUSES" MIGHT GIVE US A MENTION.

DANNY FRASIER

DIST. BY QUATERNARY FEATURES-P.O. BOX 72-NY-NY-10021

©1993 RUBEN BOLLING

NIGHT of the ZOMBIE DOCTORS

I HURT MY ANKLE PLAYING VOLLEYBALL, SO I WENT OVER TO THE EMERGENCY ROOM.

A RESIDENT IN ROOM 4A CAN SEE YOU NOW.

YES?

AAAA!!

PLEASE DON'T BE ALARMED. I'M OPERATING ON A BIT LESS SLEEP THAN I'D LIKE...

NOW, LET'S SEE... APPARENTLY...YOU ...zz...ZZZ...

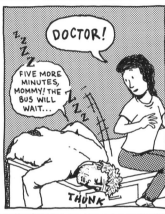

DOCTOR!

FIVE MORE MINUTES, MOMMY! THE BUS WILL WAIT...

THUNK

OH, I'M SORRY ABOUT DR. RYAN. A WEAK MAN, I'M AFRAID. WHY, HE SLEPT ONLY LAST WEEK.

THAT'S INSANE!

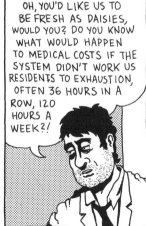

OH, YOU'D LIKE US TO BE FRESH AS DAISIES, WOULD YOU? DO YOU KNOW WHAT WOULD HAPPEN TO MEDICAL COSTS IF THE SYSTEM DIDN'T WORK US RESIDENTS TO EXHAUSTION, OFTEN 36 HOURS IN A ROW, 120 HOURS A WEEK?!

OH MY GOD! I'M GETTING OUT OF HERE!!

GET BACK HERE! WE STILL HAVE TO GET THAT APPENDIX OUT... ZZZZZ

NURSE! HAND ME MY 5 IRON!

AFRAID... ...WE... HAVE TO... OPERATE...

HOSPITAL

HOP HOP

7

TOM the DANCING BUG

©1993 RUBEN BOLLING

HARVEY **RICHARDS** Lawyer for Children

WE JOIN MR. RICHARDS ON A TYPICAL BUSY DAY.

...WHY DON'T YOU JUST DO AN "EENIE-MEENIE-MEINIE-MOE"? THAT WOULD RESOLVE THE WHOLE THING!

BECAUSE I MIGHT **LOSE**!!

LOOK, ZACK, "EENIE-MEENIE-MEINIE-MOE" ALWAYS ENDS UP WHERE YOU START IT!

IT DOES?

EXCUSE ME, STACY IS WAITING FOR YOU IN CONFERENCE ROOM B.

I'LL BE RIGHT IN.

ALSO, MR. RICHARDS, TEDDY MILLER HASN'T PAID US FOR THE WATER FOUNTAIN CASE. HE SAYS HE LOST HIS ALLOWANCE.

RIGHT. WE'LL SLAP A LIEN ON HIS NINTENDO. HE'LL COUGH IT UP.

"...AND YOU... ARE...**IT**"! HEY, HE'S **RIGHT**!

WHAT'S UP, STACY?

I BORROWED MY BROTHER'S TONKA, AND I BROKE IT. SHOULD I SAY IT WAS BROKEN WHEN I GOT IT?

LET ME TELL YOU SOMETHING ABOUT LYING, STACY. ONE LIE ALWAYS LEADS TO ANOTHER!

AND **THAT** LIE WILL LEAD TO ANOTHER AND ANOTHER...

BUT THAT'S USUALLY ABOUT IT. THREE OR FOUR LIES, TOPS, AND YOU'RE IN THE CLEAR.

OKAY, THANKS, MR. RICHARDS!

DIST. BY QUATERNARY FEATURES · P.O. BOX 72 · NY · NY · 10021

TOM the DANCING BUG

BY RUBEN BOLLING
eMAIL: TOMDBUG@AOL.COM

FOR YOUR AMUSEMENT, IT'S...

O.J. SIMPSON

THE CARTOON

MR. SIMPSON, YOU'RE UNDER SUSPICION FOR MURDER!

WHAT POSSIBLE EVIDENCE COULD YOU HAVE AGAINST ME?!

APPARENTLY, YOU DROPPED ONE BLOODY GLOVE AT THE MURDER SCENE, AND THE OTHER IN YOUR BACKYARD!

D'OH!

OKAY, BUDDY! WE'RE FUGITIVES! WHAT SHOULD WE DO?

UM...LET'S CALL THE POLICE AND SEE HOW MANY OF MY SUPPORTERS SHOW UP FOR THE CHASE!

COMING UP ON "48 MINUTES": OUR STORY ON THE COVERAGE OF THE MEDIA HYPE SURROUNDING THE REPORTING OF THE SIMPSON CHARGES!

SIMPSON COVERAGE

NOT TO WORRY-- IF YOU HIRE ME AND EVERY OTHER FAMOUS LAWYER IN THE COUNTRY... WE'LL GET YOU OFF!

WOO-HOO!

BUT WILL THEY?! TUNE IN NEXT TIME AND FIND OUT WHAT'S IN STORE FOR O.J. SIMPSON--

WILL AN ACQUITTAL ALLOW HIM TO CONTINUE HIS ENDORSEMENTS?

HURTS CAR RENTAL! FOR WHEN YOU'RE IN A RUSH AT THE AIRPORT!

GATE A-F $

CUT! BEAUTIFUL!

AND IF FOUND GUILTY, WILL HE DO HARD TIME....

DON'T YOU GUYS WANT TO HEAR FOOTBALL STORIES?

NO, NO! TELL US ABOUT YOUR ACTING CAREER!

WHAT WAS IT LIKE WORKING WITH AVA GARDNER?

OR WILL HE BE SENTENCED TO (GASP) MORE COMMUNITY SERVICE?!

COCK-TAIL, MR. SIMPSON?

NOT NOW! CAN'T YOU SEE I'M CONCENTRATING ON PAYING MY DEBT TO SOCIETY?!

©1992 Ruben Bolling

THE DICHOTOMIES OF BOB

INEXPLICABLE!

COMPLEX!

AMAZING!

WHO'S TO SAY?!

DIST. BY QUATERNARY FEATURES   P.O. BOX 72 - NY - NY - 10021

BOB DOES NOT LIKE ICED TEA WHEN IT'S BREWED.

YET BOB LIKES ICED TEA FROM A MIX.

BOB WILL EAT FOOD THAT HAS DROPPED ON THE FLOOR.

YET BOB WILL NOT EAT FOOD THAT HAS GONE INTO THE GARBAGE, EVEN IF IT'S STILL WRAPPED.

BOB WILL OFTEN RENT 3 VIDEOS AT A TIME.

YET HE HAS TO STAY UP VERY LATE TO WATCH THEM ALL.

BOB ALWAYS FOLLOWS INSTRUCTIONS.

YET, DESPITE THE INSTRUCTIONS ON THE BOX, HE WILL STICK Q-TIPS INTO HIS EAR CANAL.

WHEN BOB DOESN'T FEEL LIKE LISTENING TO ANY OF HIS TAPES, HE LISTENS TO THE RADIO.

YET WHEN HE'S FINDING A RADIO STATION, HE'LL STOP AT A STATION PLAYING A SONG ON ONE OF HIS TAPES.

AS A CHILD, BOB PREFERRED "LOST IN SPACE" TO "STAR TREK."

YET BOB NOW PREFERS "STAR TREK: THE NEXT GENERATION" TO BOTH.

BOB WATCHES "MONDAY NIGHT FOOTBALL" WHILE HE TAPES "MURPHY BROWN."

YET HE WATCHES "SATURDAY NIGHT LIVE" WHILE HE TAPES "AMERICAN GLADIATORS."

BOB DOES NOT LIKE STRAWBERRIES.

YET BOB LIKES STRAW-BERRY-FLAVORED LICORICE.

10

BY RUBEN BOLLING

TOMDBUG@AOL.COM

DIST. BY QUATERNARY FEATURES - P.O. BOX 72 - NY - NY - 10021   ©1996 R. BOLLING

Games Louis Plays.

HOW ON EARTH DID YOU GET **GUM** IN YOUR **HAIR**?

I DON'T KNOW.

Revenge Plans for Paul Kelly.

PLAN ① FINDING KELLY AFTER SCHOOL AND STARTING A FIGHT.

OKAY, KELLY! NOW YOU'RE GONNA GET IT!

ADVANTAGE: PUNCHING HIM IN THE FACE.

DISADVANTAGE: **HIM** PUNCHING **ME** IN THE FACE MUCH, MUCH MORE OFTEN.

PLAN ② LEARNING KARATE, AND **THEN** FIGHTING KELLY.

OKAY, KELLY! NOW YOU'RE GONNA GET IT!

ADVANTAGE: KICKING HIM IN THE FACE.

DISADVANTAGE: A LOT OF WORK, AND HE'D **STILL** PROBABLY BEAT ME UP.

PLAN ③ SETTING A BAG OF DOG CRAP ON FIRE AT HIS DOORSTEP AND RINGING THE DOORBELL.

HEY!

STAMP STAMP

ADVANTAGE: HE'D NEVER KNOW FOR **SURE** IT WAS ME.

DISADVANTAGE: HE'D PROBABLY **GUESS** IT WAS ME AND BEAT ME UP **ANYWAY**.

PLAN ④ WAITING YEARS AND YEARS-- UNTIL KELLY HAS FORGOTTEN ALL ABOUT ME--AND **THEN** GETTING REVENGE!

I DON'T GET IT! SOMEONE'S BEEN CHUCKING EGGS AT MY HOUSE, STICKING POTATOES IN MY TAIL PIPE, ORDERING PIZZAS TO MY ADDRESS... BUT **WHO?!** IT'S RUINING MY LIFE!!

AH, YOU'RE A LOSER, MR. KELLY.

ADVANTAGE: ZERO CHANCE OF GETTING BEAT UP.

DISADVANTAGE: YEARS AND YEARS FROM NOW I'LL BE GROWN UP AND I PROBABLY WON'T **WANT** TO GET REVENGE ANYMORE.

SO I **SOLEMNLY SWEAR** THAT **ONE DAY**, I WILL GET EVEN WITH PAUL KELLY --EVEN IF I DON'T FEEL LIKE IT ANYMORE!

TOM THE DANCING BUG

©1993 RUBEN BOLLING

AN AUSTRALOPITHECINE WITH A JOB.

YES, CHARLEY HAS FOUND HIMSELF GAINFUL EMPLOYMENT!

MY OWN CUBICLE! MAN, IT PAYS TO PAD YOUR RESUMÉ!

AT THE WATER COOLER, CHARLEY INSTINCTIVELY TAKES CAUTIOUS SIPS AS HE FURTIVELY SCANS THE HALLWAYS FOR SUPERIORS.

PREDATORS ALWAYS PICK YOU OFF AT THE WATERING HOLE.

THEN IT'S BACK TO WORK, WORK, WORK.

THIS PAPER LOOKS LIKE IT SHOULD GO HERE, THIS ONE MAYBE SHOULD BE PUT IN AN ENVELOPE, I'LL THROW THIS ONE OUT...

BEFORE LONG, IT'S TIME FOR A COFFEE BREAK.

HEY, YOU **ATE** ALL THE NON-DAIRY CREAMER!

OH...SORRY! THERE'S PLENTY OF THIS "WHITE-OUT" STUFF LEFT-- I DIDN'T LIKE THAT.

CHARLEY COMMITS AN OFFICE FAUX PAS WHEN HE'S A BIT TOO HEAVY ON THE MEN'S ROOM BANTER.

SAY, MR. KARP, DID YOU CATCH "FULL HOUSE" LAST NIGHT?

BUT CHARLEY'S FINAL BLUNDER IS GETTING CAUGHT USING THE COPY MACHINE FOR IMPROPER PURPOSES.

HOW DO YOU KNOW IT WAS **ME**?

WHO **ELSE** COULD HAVE A BUTT **THIS** HAIRY?

AT LEAST I MADE IT OUT OF THERE WITH SOME OFFICE SUPPLIES.

DIST. BY QUATERNARY FEATURES-P.O. BOX 72-NY-NY-10021

13

TOM the DANCING BUG

BY RUBEN BOLLING

DIST BY QUATERNARY FEATURES · P.O. BOX 72 · NY· NY· 10021 · ©1994 RUBEN BOLLING

EMAIL: TOMDBUG@AOL.COM

NATURAL HABITATS

TODAY ON "NATURAL HABITATS" WE TAKE A LOOK AT A WONDEROUS CREATURE TO WHOM WE ALL OWE A DEBT OF GRATITUDE!

BEHOLD THE *NATURALLY UNEMPLOYED WORKER!!*

ECONOMISTS BELIEVE THERE IS A "NATURAL" RATE OF UNEMPLOYMENT--ABOUT 6%-- WHICH MUST EXIST TO WARD OFF INFLATION.

EXCUSE ME, WOULD YOU LIKE A JOB?

YES! I **NEED** ONE!

♪ It's ♪ the story ♪ of a lovely lady...

WANT ADS

HA, HA! ISN'T THAT CUTE?! OF **COURSE** HE DOES--THAT'S THE **NATURE** OF THESE MISBEGOTTEN BRUTES!

CAN NATURE BE CRUEL? NO DOUBT. ARE THESE CREATURES UNSIGHTLY? YOU BET.

YET WE MUST REPRESS OUR REVULSION, KEEPING IN MIND THEIR PART IN THE DELICATE BALANCE OF OUR ECONOMY.

SO REMEMBER--THE FED IS KEEPING UNEMPLOYMENT UP AT 6% BECAUSE ... IT'S *ONLY NATURAL!!*

Need Job! Call Me!

THE INEFFICIENCY OF BEING MALE

EXAMPLE #83

2 GLASSES OF WINE

1 PITCHER OF BEER

1 PITCHER OF BEER

1 PITCHER OF BEER

1 PITCHER OF BEER

TOTAL BAR BILL: $8.00 $36.00

BY THE ARTIST FORMERLY KNOWN AS RUBEN BOLLING

IT'S A REVOLUTION.

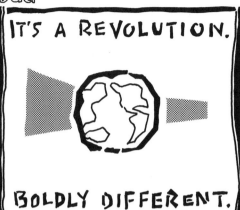

BOLDLY DIFFERENT.

IT DOESN'T PLAY BY RULES IT DOESN'T BELIEVE IN.

IT'S FUN-LOVING,

BUT SERIOUS-MINDED.

IT CAN BREAK DOWN WALLS OF INJUSTICE.

IT BRINGS A HOLISTIC MESSAGE OF PEACE AND TRANSCENDENTAL LOVE.

IT'S HI-HO™ FRUIT DRINK

"SAME OLD FRUCTOSE WATER, BUT NOW WITH A GROOVY NEW MARKETING STRATEGY"

FROM HI-HO BEVERAGES, LTD., A DIVISION OF CHEM-A-COLA, INC., A WHOLLY-OWNED SUBSIDIARY OF NERREX CORP.

TOM the DANCING BUG

©1993 RUBEN BOLLING

MALIBU FIREFIGHTERS

THE WILDFIRES OF '93

CAPTAIN! THE WINDS ARE BLOWING THE BRUSHFIRES WESTWARD!

GOOD LORD! THAT PUTS THEM ON TRACK TO HIT **BOB NEWHART'S** AND **DICK VAN DYKE'S** HOUSES!

ALERT THE COPTERS AND PLANES! I WANT RETARDANT ALL OVER THE WESTERN PASS. WE'LL PUSH THIS THING TO THE SOUTH!

WHAT ABOUT ALL THESE HOUSES TO THE SOUTH?

JUST A BUNCH OF AGENTS AND PUBLICISTS, NO PROBLEM.

WAIT. THAT'S **MARK HAMILL'S** HOUSE THERE!

DAMN! "**STAR WARS**" IS A CLASSIC, AND HE DESERVES RESPECT EVEN IF HE **IS** ONLY MARGINALLY TALENTED!

I SAY WE **LET** IT GO WEST. I'VE SEEN RERUNS OF THE BOB NEWHART SHOW, AND FRANKLY IT HASN'T HELD UP.

HEY, PAL! *THE DICK VAN DYKE SHOW! MARY POPPINS?* WE'VE GOT SOME TOUGH CHOICES TO MAKE, BUT VAN DYKE'S HOUSE IS TO THE WEST, AND IT'S NOT **TOUCHED**, CAPICHE?!

CAP, THIS IS MULLER IN CHOPPER 3. WHY NOT PUSH IT TO THE **SOUTHWEST**?

BECAUSE **SEAN PENN'S** HOUSE WOULD BE FRIED! HE'S ONE OF OUR MOST TALENTED YOUNG ACTORS.

WELL, SURE HE'S **FAMOUS** -- HE MARRIED MADONNA. BUT PERHAPS IT'S TIME TO CONSIDER WHETHER HE'S **OVERRATED** AS AN ACTOR! HE'S NEVER REALLY TOUCHED THE BRILLIANCE HE SHOWED IN "**FAST TIMES**"!

YOU KNOW, HE'S RIGHT! "SHANGHAI SURPRISE," "WE'RE NO ANGELS"... HOW LONG CAN HE COAST ON HIS INTENSE METHOD ACTOR REP?!

BUT WHAT ABOUT HIS PROMISING DIRECTORIAL DEBUT IN "**INDIAN RUNNER**"?!

PONDEROUS AND WITHOUT ANY SENSE OF IRONY.

IT GOES SOUTHWEST. PENN BEARS THE BRUNT.

MOVE IT OUT!

DIST. BY QUATERNARY FEATURES · P.O. BOX 72 · NY·NY·10021

by RUBEN BOLLING
TOMDBUG@AOL.COM
DIST. BY QUATERNARY FEATURES—©1996 R. BOLLING

NEWS of the TIMES

POLITICAL PRICE-WAR TO BENEFIT CONSUMERS

FIERCE PRICING COMPETITION BETWEEN THE TWO POLITICAL PARTIES IS EXPECTED TO BE A BOON TO CONSUMERS OF POLITICAL PRODUCTS THROUGHOUT THE FALL.

J J A S O N D

RONALD ERIKSEN, C.E.O. OF GLOMCO, INC.:

A RIDER TO A BILL... LET'S SAY AN **ENVIRONMENTAL EXEMPTION** OR A **TAX LOOPHOLE**... USED TO COST ME A FEW MILLION. NOW I CAN GET ONE FOR **$500,000** EASY!

DEMOCRATIC PARTY SPOKESMAN ROBERT HAMELIN:

FROM **LOW-LEVEL** BRIBES TO **LOCAL OFFICIALS** ALL THE WAY UP TO THE **PRESIDENT'S EAR** ON AN AIR FORCE ONE EXCURSION, ... **WE'RE SLASHING PRICES!**

Democrat ☆96☆

REPUBLICAN PARTY SPOKESMAN PETER DeFALCO:

OUR PRICES ARE SO LOW, WE'RE PRACTICALLY **GIVING AWAY** THE PUBLIC TRUST!

WE MUST BE INSANE!!

POLITICAL INDUSTRY ANALYST JASON WARNER EXPLAINS THE PRICE-WAR:

AS THE DIFFERENCES BETWEEN THE PARTIES DISAPPEAR, AND THEY BOTH OFFER ESSENTIALLY THE SAME POLITICAL PHILOSOPHY, CONSUMERS' PRICE SENSITIVITY BECOMES MUCH GREATER.

THE LEADERS OF THE TWO PARTIES SQUARED OFF RECENTLY BEFORE AN AUDIENCE OF **CORPORATE AND LOBBYING EXECUTIVES.**

THE DEMOCRATS MAY HAVE MATCHED OUR PRICES, BUT THEY CAN'T OFFER THE **TOTAL COMMITMENT TO SELLING OUT** THAT WE DO!

YOU CAN'T BEAT THE DEMOCRATS FOR THAT **"THE CUSTOMER IS ALWAYS RIGHT"** ATTITUDE!

DIST. BY QUATERNARY FEATURES · P.O. BOX 72 · N.Y. · N.Y. · 10021

©1995 R. BOLLING

THE ADVENTURES OF

SAM ROLAND

THE DETECTIVE WHO DIES

THE MYSTERY OF THE TAP-DANCING MUMMY

AT THE CENTRAL CITY MUSEUM--

WE APPRECIATE YOUR TAKING ON THIS CASE, MR. ROLAND!

GLAD TO HELP!

I JUST DON'T UNDER-STAND HOW-- OR **WHY** ANYONE WOULD STEAL A MUMMY!

WELL, IT DIDN'T JUST **WALK** AWAY!

NO, IT **TAP-DANCED!**

AH, THIS IS THE NIGHT JANITOR, SVENSEN. HE CLAIMS TO HAVE HEARD **TAP-DANCING** LAST NIGHT!

AND I FOUND **THIS** A FEW YARDS FROM THE EXHIBIT!

THIS MIGHT BE A CLUE! I THINK I'LL PAY A LITTLE VISIT!

Abandoned Warehouse

234 Clifford St.

ON ROLAND'S ARRIVAL AT THE WARE-HOUSE, HE FINDS HIMSELF THE SUBJECT OF GUNFIRE!

WELL, **THIS** IS SUSPICIOUS!

BANG!? BANG!

*PING!

*PING!

A PLAN QUICKLY FORMULATES IN ROLAND'S MIND.

THAT CRATE SUSPENDED OVER HIS HEAD....

BANG

HMM... IT'S DANGEROUS, BUT IT **JUST MIGHT WORK!**

HE LUNGES TO RELEASE THE ROPE HOLDING UP THE DANGLING CARRIER...

...BUT IS SHOT AND KILLED INSTANTLY!

AAA..

BANG

THE MYSTERY OF THE TAP-DANCING MUMMY MAY ONE DAY BE SOLVED, BUT IT WON'T BE BY **SAM ROLAND, THE DETECTIVE WHO DIES!**

Games Louis Plays: Waiting for the Swamp Monster.

ANY SECOND, THE SWAMP MONSTER IS GOING TO CRASH THROUGH THAT WINDOW.

HE'S GONNA JUMP IN AND SNAP MY NECK BEFORE I CAN EVEN YELL FOR HELP.

WAIT A MINUTE. THE SWAMP MONSTER ISN'T REAL. HE'S JUST FROM A MADE-UP MOVIE.

BESIDES, EVEN IF THERE WAS A SWAMP MONSTER, WHY WOULD HE COME AFTER ME?

THERE ARE MILLIONS OF OTHER PEOPLE WHO THE SWAMP MONSTER COULD ATTACK.

AND A LOT OF THEM LIVE MUCH CLOSER TO SWAMPS THAN I DO.

I MEAN, WOULDN'T IT BE TOO MUCH OF A COINCIDENCE THAT HE WOULD CRASH THROUGH MY WINDOW ON THE SAME NIGHT I WATCHED THE MOVIE ABOUT HIM?

ANY SECOND, THE SWAMP MONSTER IS GOING TO CRASH THROUGH THAT WINDOW.

20

BY RUBEN BOLLING

THE EVOLUTIONARY PSYCHOLOGY OF LOVE

Panel 1

NICE PARTY, HUH?

HI. YES, IT IS.

Panel 2

AS A HUMAN FEMALE, I CAN PHYSICALLY PRODUCE ONLY ONE OFFSPRING A YEAR, SO IT'S TO MY GENETIC ADVANTAGE TO LOOK FOR A **RELIABLE** PARTNER WITH WHOM TO PAIR-BOND.

Panel 3

AS A HUMAN **MALE**, I CAN PRODUCE **MANY** OFFSPRING, SO IT'S TO MY GENETIC ADVANTAGE TO TAKE **ANY** OPPORTUNITY TO PROCREATE.

Panel 4

GIVEN MY HUGE PHYSICAL INVESTMENT IN REPRODUCTION, I WILL NOT MATE WITHOUT FIRST TAKING TIME TO MAKE SURE THAT A POTENTIAL PARTNER HAS THE ABILITY AND INCLINATION TO SHARE IN PARENTING.

Panel 5

I MAY AS WELL SPEND THAT TIME **ACTING** AS THOUGH I HAVE THE MAKINGS OF A GOOD PARENT, WHILE FOR THE TIME BEING REALLY ONLY LOOKING FOR A FIT (ATTRACTIVE) FEMALE WITH WHOM TO MATE.

Panel 6

...SO, YOU WANT TO GET A CUP OF COFFEE OR SOMETHING?

I WAS JUST THINKING THE SAME, EXACT THING.

DIST. BY QUATERNARY FEATURES- P.O. BOX 72-N.Y.-N.Y.-10021- EMAIL: TOMBUG@AOL.COM

TOM the DANCING BUG

BY RUBEN BOLLING
TOMDBUG@AOL.COM

The Day They Made Murder Legal.

- a parable -

ONE DAY, MURDER WAS LEGALIZED. WE ARE INEXPLICABLY MAKING MURDER LEGAL, FOR THE PURPOSES OF THIS PARABLE.

O.K.

MOST PEOPLE STILL DID NOT MURDER. ALTHOUGH IT WOULD BE LEGAL FOR ME TO KILL YOU, I WILL NOT-- FOR I AM A GOOD PERSON WITH AN INTERNALIZED MORAL CODE.

THANK YOU.

BUT THERE ARE "PERSONS" WHO ROAM THE EARTH THAT ARE NOT HUMAN--THEY ARE MADE-UP ENTITIES CALLED "CORPORATIONS."

I RUN INC.-CO. ON BEHALF OF ITS SHAREHOLDERS WHO HAVE GIVEN ME ONE DIRECTIVE: MAKE PROFITS.

A PERSON RUNNING A CORPORATION DECIDED TO MURDER BECAUSE IT WOULD INCREASE PROFITS.

YOU ARE INC-CO'S COMPETITION.

OW! YOU KILLED ME!

BANG!

AT FIRST, PEOPLE WERE MAD AT THE CORPORATION AND ITS DIRECTOR.

YOU'RE A BAD ENTITY. YOU COMMITTED AN ACT WHICH, ALTHOUGH LEGAL, IS MORALLY EVIL.

INC.-CO.

INC-CO BAD

BOO INC-CO

BUT AN EXPLANATION WAS AT HAND... I PERSONALLY WOULD NEVER COMMIT MURDER, BUT IN MY CAPACITY AS CORPORATE DIRECTOR, I HAD TO!

MY FIDUCIARY DUTY IS TO DO ANYTHING WITHIN THE LAW TO MAXIMIZE PROFITS FOR THE CORPORATION!

IT WOULD BE IMMORAL FOR ME NOT TO KILL!

AND SO IT WAS THAT CORPORATIONS DID BAD THINGS THAT GOOD PEOPLE WOULD NOT.

MASSIVE LAY-OFFS

AREN'T YOU GLAD THIS IS JUST A MAKE-BELIVE PARABLE?

DIST. BY QUATERNARY FEATURES ©1996 R. BOLLING

TOM
THE
DANCING
BUG

BY
RUBEN
BOLLING
EMAIL: TOMDBUG@AOL.COM

DIST. BY QUATERNARY FEATURES · P.O. BOX 72 · NY · NY · 10021   ©1995 R. BOLLING

JAPAN TO WORLD: "SORRY ABOUT W.W.II!"

APOLOGIZING'S ALL THE RAGE...
BUT WHY WAIT FIFTY YEARS?

WHAT A WAY TO WIPE THE SLATE CLEAN! WITH ONE MONDO MEA CULPA, YOU'RE EXONERATED FOR WHATEVER HORRORS MAY HAVE BEEN INFLICTED!

For a limited time only, the **WORLD'S BEST** APOLOGIZER is now available to deliver your expression of regret! YES, **HUGH GRANT** will be adorably contrite on <u>your</u> behalf!

JUST LOOK AT WHAT HUGH COULD DO...

FOR THE MOST APPEALING APOLOGIES, ALLOWING YOUR NATION OR ETHNIC GROUP TO <u>MOVE ON</u>,   *CALL TODAY!!*

THE "TOM THE DANCING BUG" COMIC STRIP Presents...

AN AMERICAN RITE OF PASSAGE

WRITTEN AND ILLUSTRATED BY: RUBEN BOLLING
TOMDBUG@AOL.COM

DIST. BY QUATERNARY FEATURES—P.O. BOX 72—N.Y.—N.Y.—10021

© 1994 RUBEN BOLLING

25

Tom the Dancing Bug

©1992 Ruben Bolling

I'VE TRIED TO FIGHT IT, BUT I GUESS I'LL HAVE TO ADMIT IT-- I'M GAY!

HOLD ON, *FRIEND!* DON'T GIVE UP THE FIGHT! *SCIENCE* HAS GIVEN YOU A SOLUTION!

WE ALL KNOW THAT HOMOSEXUALITY IS **UNNATURAL** AND IMMORAL! MANY OF OUR NATION'S LEADERS HAVE SAID SO! BUT WITH AN AMAZING NEW PRODUCT, *YOU CAN BE CURED!*

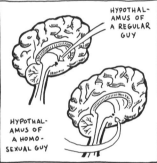

HERE'S HOW IT WORKS: YOU SEE, HOMOSEXUALS HAVE A SMALLER **ANTERERIOR HYPOTHALAMUS** THAN HETEROSEXUALS!

HYPOTHALAMUS OF A REGULAR GUY

HYPOTHALAMUS OF A HOMOSEXUAL GUY

ALL THESE FELLOWS NEED IS A FEW EXTRA HYPOTHALAMUS CELLS. HERE'S A TYPICAL HOMOSEXUAL.

FEH.

WE JUST PLACE SOME HYPOTHALAMUS-HELPER™ BRAND HYPOTHALAMUS CELLS INTO THE BRAIN...

MORE HYPOTHALAMUS-HELPER, NURSE.

AND JUST LOOK AT THE RESULTS!

HUBBA HUBBA!

YOW!

BOYNG!

YES! BY ALTERING THE BRAIN STRUCTURE WITH HIGH-TECH BIOENGINEERED MATERIAL, WE CAN MAKE BEHAVIOR MORE... **NATURAL!**

SUDDENLY I HAVE THE URGE TO WEAR TACKY PANTS AND GO BOWLING.

IF GOD HAD INTENDED THERE TO BE HOMOSEXUALS, HE WOULDN'T HAVE GIVEN US THE ABILITY TO MAKE:

HYPOTHALAMUS HELPER

INSERT IN BRAIN

ASK YOUR DOCTOR!

ALSO AVAILABLE IN A PATCH!

COMING SOON-- A CURE FOR CIVIL UNREST: **WHITENESS HELPER™** BRAND SKIN LIGHTENING TREATMENTS (EVER NOTICE HOW DOCILE MICHAEL JACKSON IS?)

QUATERNARY FEATURES-P.O. BOX 72-NY-NY-10021

26

TOM the DANCING BUG

BY RUBEN BOLLING
EMAIL: TOMDBUG@AOL.COM
DIST. BY QUATERNARY FEATURES · P.O. BOX 72 · NY · NY · 10021
© 1995 R. BOLLING

THE ADVENTURES OF

SAM ROLAND
THE DETECTIVE WHO DIES

THE CASE OF THE FUCHSIA PARROT

WEALTHY MRS. VAN HAAM'S PRICELESS FUCHSIA PARROT IS DISCOVERED MISSING, AND SAM ROLAND IS CALLED IN.

HMM...DO YOU HAVE ANY ENEMIES, MRS. VAN HAAM?

WELL, I RECENTLY FIRED MY BUTLER, AND HE THREATENED TO GET EVEN WITH ME.

THE ILL-FATED INVESTIGATOR DECIDES TO INQUIRE AT THE FORMER BUTLER'S ADDRESS...

IS MRS. VAN HAAM'S EX-BUTLER HERE?

KNOCK KNOCK

WHO WANTS TO KNOW?

SUDDENLY -- A BLOW TO THE HEAD!

POW

IS THIS THE END FOR SAM ROLAND, THE DETECTIVE WHO DIES?!

NO! NOT YET!

WHAT TH...

AH, MR. ROLAND. YOU WOKE UP JUST IN TIME. HOPE YOU DON'T MIND IF I DON'T STAY TO CHAT!

YOU SEE, IN ONE MINUTE, WATER WILL COME FLOWING INTO THIS CHAMBER, DROWNING YOU LIKE A RAT!

TA-TA!

ROLAND QUICKLY GETS TO WORK!

IF I CAN JUST LOOSEN THESE ROPES...

MAYBE IF I EXPAND MY LUNGS...

AH...BY SHIFTING MY CHAIR, I CAN...

AND SO THE CASE OF THE FUCHSIA PARROT IS ENTERED IN THE BOOKS AS ANOTHER CASE LEFT UNSOLVED BY SAM ROLAND, THE DETECTIVE WHO DIES!

BY RUBEN BOLLING

TOMDBUG@AOL.COM

DIST. BY QUATERNARY FEATURES. P.O. BOX 72. NY. NY. 10021

©1996 R. BOLLING

Police Dept. Story

MY **GUT** TELLS ME THAT **STEVENS** IS THE MURDERER, BUT DAMMIT, WE DON'T HAVE ENOUGH TO **CONVICT!**

BUT LIEUTENANT! HE WAS **AT** THE SCENE OF THE MURDER AND **RAN** WHEN OFFICER JONES APPROACHED!

COME ON! HE COULD HAVE BEEN A **BYSTANDER** WHO JUSTIFIABLY REGARDS ALL POLICE AS A **CORRUPT** AND ABUSIVE **THREAT!**

SO THE MURDER WEAPON FOUND ON STEVENS WHEN JONES CAUGHT UP TO HIM WOULD BE... *INADMISSIBLE!*

BUT HIS FINGER-PRINTS AND D.N.A. ALL OVER THE WEAPON AND VICTIM...

ANY JURY WOULD FIND THEY WERE **PLANTED** BY **US!**

RING!

LIEUTENANT! WE **NAILED** STEVENS! WE FOUND TWO SEPARATE VIDEOTAPES AND DOZENS OF SNAPSHOTS OF HIM COMMITING THE MURDER!

THINK, MAN! WE COULD HAVE **FORGED** THOSE! IT JUST **WON'T STICK!**

WE'RE LETTING YOU GO, STEVENS.

EVERYTHING WE HAVE ON YOU IS TAINTED BY OUR OWN CORRUPTION

BUT... I **DID** IT!

OH, HE'S A SLIPPERY ONE. PLAYS THE SYSTEM LIKE A FIDDLE.

BUT SOONER OR LATER HE'LL MAKE A MISTAKE...

AND WE'LL BE THERE!

NEXT WEEK: 60,000 EYEWITNESSES COME FORWARD!

"NO JURY WOULD CONVICT-- WE COULD HAVE PAID THEM OFF. WE NEED *MORE!*"

BOB DOLE'S VISION of AMERICA'S FUTURE

by RUBEN BOLLING

email: TOMDBUG@AOL.COM

"ELECT ME, AND I'LL USE *MODERN SCIENCE* TO USHER IN THE NEW MILLENNIUM!"

DIST. BY QUATERNARY FEATURES · P.O.BOX 72-NY-NY-10021 · ©1996 R. BOLLING

DON'T WANT TO MISS A TELEVISION PROGRAM WHEN YOU GO OUT TO THE CLUB? A **V.C.R.** ("VICARIOUS COMMUNICATOR ROBOT") WILL WATCH THE PROGRAM, THEN TELL YOU ALL ABOUT IT WHEN YOU COME HOME!

AND THEN HOSS SAID TO LITTLE JOE...

CRUISE DOWN SPACIOUS FREEWAYS IN ROOMY AUTOMOBILES! WORRIED ABOUT GASOLINE MILEAGE? FANCY "**COMPUTING MACHINES**" ON BOARD WILL MAKE THESE VEHICLES COMFORTABLE **AND** EFFICIENT!

BY MY SECOND TERM, THE HOUSEWIFE OF THE FUTURE WILL MAKE BUTTER WITH AN **AUTOMATED MACHINE**, MAKING **THE BUTTER CHURN** A THING OF THE PAST!

Butter-Matic

BUSY BUSINESSMEN MAY NOT HAVE TIME TO COME TO WASHINGTON, D.C. TO TELL ME WHAT TO DO... NEW-FANGLED "**VOICE-CONVEYORS**" WILL ALLOW INSTANTANEOUS COMMUNICATION!

HELLO, PRES. DOLE? THERE ARE SOME PESTY E.P.A. PEOPLE HERE I WANT TAKEN CARE OF.

THE END... OR THE BEGINNING?

TOM the DANCING BUG BY RUBEN BOLLING

eMAIL: TOMDBUG@AOL.COM

HARVEY RICHARDS *Lawyer for Children*

1-800-KKIDLAW
THE EXTRA "K" IS FOR EXTRA KOUNSEL

...SO I ASK HIM TO SEND ME A RETAINER, AND THE BRAT MAILS ME **THIS** SLOBBERY THING!

MR. RICHARDS, JOEY KIRK IS ON LINE 2. TROUBLE AT THE ELM PLAYGROUND!

TELL HIM I'LL BE RIGHT THERE!

WHAT'S THE PROBLEM, JOEY.

I FOUND THIS COOL OLD TRUCK BEHIND THAT FENCE!

BUT LARRY O'NEIL SAYS IT'S **HIS!** HE'S JUST A BIG, FAT **LIAR!**

ORDINARILY, I'D SAY THAT EVEN IF THE TRUCK **WAS** HIS, UNDER THE "FINDER'S KEEPERS, LOSERS WEEPERS" DOCTRINE, IT'S NOW LAWFULLY YOURS!

RIGHT! IT'S AN OPEN AND SHUT CASE!

BUT IN THIS CASE, I ADVISE YOU TO **HAND THE TRUCK OVER TO HIM!**

WHAT?

LOOK AT HIM, JOEY! HE'S A **BRUTE!** HE'LL POUND YOU INTO **PULP!**

A LAWYER MUST CONSIDER NOT ONLY **LEGAL** FACTORS, BUT **PRACTICAL** ONES AS WELL...AND I'D SAY YOU'D BETTER GIVE THAT TRUCK TO LARRY **NOW!**

THAT'S NOT FAIR!

NEED I CITE THE CLASSIC DOCTRINE, **"LIFE'S NOT FAIR!"**

I'LL SEND YOU MY BILL...

30

—BY—
RUBEN "DUDE" BOLLING

email: TOMDBUG@AOL.COM

DudeSpeak

Translated.

"GREETINGS, FRIEND." "GREETINGS."

"YOUR GOATEE IS GROWING IN VERY WELL." "THANK YOU."

"WHAT DO YOU THINK OF THE TREND OF REGARDING NIETZSCHE AS A DIALECTICIAN?"

"WHOLLY MISGUIDED. NIETZSCHE INVESTIGATED FORCES AND THEIR OBJECTS, BUT DID NOT VIEW ONE AS A NEGATIVE ELEMENT IN THE ESSENCE OF THE OTHER."

"I HOPE TO SPEAK WITH YOU AGAIN SOON." "COOL."

DIST. BY QUATERNARY FEATURES · PO BOX 72 · NY-NY-10021 · ©1994 RUBEN BOLLING

TOM THE DANCING BUG

©1993 RUBEN BOLLING

Louis Maltby's Guide to HALLOWEEN

FIRST STEP: DITCH YOUR JACKET IN THE BUSHES!

HEY, I'M SUPPOSED TO LOOK LIKE SPIDER-MAN, NOT WHAT SPIDER-MAN WOULD LOOK LIKE IF HIS MOM MADE HIM WEAR A JACKET!

FULL FACE MASKS ARE COOLEST, BUT BEWARE OF THE DISGUSTING SALIVA POOL THAT BUILDS UP AROUND THE MOUTH.

YECH.

START EARLY! NOT ONLY DO YOU GET A HEAD START, BUT YOU NEVER KNOW WHEN YOU'RE GOING TO RUN INTO SOMETHING LIKE THIS...

We had to go out for the evening. Please take ONE

YOU'VE GOT UNTIL 8:30 TO GET AS MUCH CANDY AS POSSIBLE. THIS IS SERIOUS BUSINESS-- THERE'S NO TIME FOR FUN.

COMMUNICATION WITH YOUR FELLOW TRICK-OR-TREATERS IS VERY IMPORTANT. IT WON'T BE LONG BEFORE CELLULAR PHONES REVOLUTIONIZE THE WHOLE BUSINESS.

SWEET TARTS AND SNICKERS? SO, ATHENS DRIVE IS DEFINITELY WORTH A SIDE TRIP...

TREAT CHART (IN DESCENDING ORDER OF DESIRABILITY)

ACTUAL CANDY BARS	ONCE WORD GETS OUT, HOUSE WILL RUN OUT IN AN HOUR.
FUN-SIZE CANDY BARS, PACKS OF BUBBLE GUM	GOOD, SOLID TREATS. HIT THESE HOUSES EARLY, AND YOU CAN TAKE OFF YOUR MASK AND GO BACK AGAIN LATER.
HOME BAKED GOODS	YOU AREN'T ALLOWED TO EAT THESE (POSSIBLE POISONING), SO DON'T BRING THESE HOME. EAT THEM WHILE YOU'RE OUT.
LOLLIPOPS AND SMARTIES	CHEAPSKATE HOUSES
BAGS OF CANDY CORN	CANDY CORN AT HALLOWEEN IS LIKE SNOW AT CHRISTMAS. TOO DAMN MUCH OF THE STUFF FOR IT TO HAVE ANY VALUE.
BOXES OF RAISINS	YOU CAN GET THIS AT HOME JUST BY ASKING FOR IT.
APPLES	YOU AREN'T ALLOWED TO EAT THESE (RAZORBLADES), BUT WHO WANTS TO ANYWAY? BRING THESE HOME TO SHOW YOUR PARENTS THAT YOU WERE CAREFUL.

DIST. BY QUATERNARY FEATURES—P.O. BOX 72—NY—NY—10021

NOVEMBER 1, 7:20 A.M. THE MORAL CRISIS:

I KNOW I COLLECTED THIS MONEY FOR UNICEF, BUT... MY GOD... THE THINGS I COULD DO WITH THIS $3.87!

TOM the DANCING BUG

DIST. BY QUATERNARY FEATURES - P.O. BOX 72-NY-NY-10021

NEWS of the TIMES

CAMPAIGN
HEATS
UP OVER
SCIENTIFIC
NEWS ITEM

A REPORT ISSUED YESTERDAY THAT AN **ASTEROID** WILL **COLLIDE WITH THE EARTH** NEXT MONTH CAUSED A **POLITICAL FUROR** IN THIS CAMPAIGN SEASON. **REPUBLICANS** IMMEDIATELY CAPITALIZED ON THE NEWS.

THIS IS JUST ANOTHER EXAMPLE OF WHERE CLINTON IS LEADING THIS NATION AND THE PLANET ON WHICH IT IS SITUATED.

DEMOCRATS WERE QUICK TO PUT THEIR OWN SPIN ON THE REVELATION.

THIS ASTEROID HAD BEEN ON COLLISION COURSE WELL BEFORE CLINTON TOOK OFFICE. CERTAINLY WHILE BUSH WAS PRESIDENT, AND QUITE PROBABLY DURING REAGAN'S TERMS.

YET CLINTON MOST LIKELY WILL TAKE BLAME. FURTHER, THE ASTEROID--SIX MILES IN DIAMETER AND HURTLING TOWARD EARTH AT 45,000mph-- WILL HIT BEFORE ELECTION DAY, WHICH SHOULD CAUSE A LOW VOTER TURN-OUT, TRADITIONALLY A REPUBLICAN ADVANTAGE.

POLITICAL ANALYST BENJAMIN VALLUCCI:

IF THE IMMINENT COLLISION LEADS TO A REPUBLICAN VICTORY, IT COULD ACTUALLY BE A DISASTER FOR THE G.O.P. ...

VALLUCCI CONTINUED, "THEY WOULD HAVE A FOUR-YEAR REIGN OVER A NATION WHOLLY DEVOID OF LIFE, SAVE SOME PLANT AND INSECT SPECIES. THIS WILL SLOW G.N.P. GROWTH AND POISE THE DEMOCRATS FOR 2000."

SINCE THE NEWS, THE POLLS HAVE BEEN INCONCLUSIVE, WITH MOST RESPONDENTS UNINTERESTED IN ANSWERING POLITICAL QUESTIONS, INSTEAD GATHERING WITH FAMILY AND LOVED ONES TO WEEP.

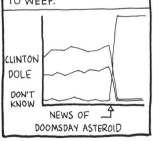

CLINTON
DOLE
DON'T KNOW

NEWS OF DOOMSDAY ASTEROID

BUT IT IS BELIEVED THAT CLINTON'S LEAD SUFFERED, AND HE TOOK SWIFT ACTION.

I HAVE REQUESTED SEVERAL HIGH-LEVEL RESIGNATIONS AND I CONSIDER THIS ASTEROID THING BEHIND US.

WE WANT TO GET BACK TO THE ISSUES AMERICANS **CARE** ABOUT.

DIST. BY QUATERNARY FEATURES ~©1996 R.BOLLING

DISNEY, THE MEDIA CONGLOMORATE THAT TRANSFORMED THE HUNCHBACK OF NOTRE DAME, A DARK AND COMPLEX NOVEL, INTO A HAPPY-MEAL-READY, FUN-FILLED FAIRY TALE, NOW PLANS THESE FUTURE BLOCKBUSTERS BASED ON LITERATURE'S CLASSICS, COMING TO A MULTIPLEX AND DISNEY RETAIL OUTLET NEAR YOU!

DISNEY'S THE TRIAL

WHAT DID I DOOO?

JOE TRIUMPHS OVER EVIL BUREAUCRATS WITH THE HELP OF HIS ANIMAL PALS, RATSY AND COO!

DISNEY'S DAS KAPITAL

POOR KARL IS LONELY AND MISUNDERSTOOD...

...SO HE USES HIS SPUNKY IMAGINATION TO DREAM UP A NEW ECONOMIC SYSTEM!

DISNEY'S HEART OF DARKNESS

WATCH OUT, MARLOW! YOU'VE GOT TO SAVE YOUR PAL KURTZ IN THE WILD CONGO!

A MUSICAL ADVENTURE THAT WILL WARM YOUR HEART!

DISNEY'S NAKED LUNCH

WILLIE'S IN THE INTERZONE, A TOPSY-TURVY WONDERLAND OF FUN! HOW WILL HE GET OUT... AND WILL HE WANT TO?!

TOM
the dancing BUG

BY RUBEN BOLLING
EMAIL: TOMDBUG@AOL.COM

DIST. BY QUATERNARY FEATURES · P.O. BOX 72 · NY-NY-10021 · ©1996 RUBEN BOLLING

ON THE ROAD AHEAD
by Bill "Kerouac" Gates

An autobiographical novel of self-discovery from the spokesman of the "Byte Generation"

I HUNGERED TO TRAVEL AMERICA, TO KNOW ITS DREAMS AND SECRETS, SO I GRABBED MY P.C. AND BEGAN MY ADVENTURE ON THE VAST, SPRAWLING ROAD!

HERE WE GO! LOOK OUT! HUP, HUP!

I BEGAN MY JOURNEY AT HTTP://WWW.AMERICASURF.COM AND QUICKLY MET A HIPSTER WHO HAD VIDEOTAPED AND CATALOGED EVERY EPISODE OF "LOIS AND CLARK" AND "THE X-FILES."

YES, YES, YES! DIG IT!!

KLIK KLIK

BUT I NEEDED TO GET ON THAT HIGHWAY AND MOVE, MAN, MOVE! SO I BUZZED OVER TO THE NEWS-GROUP ALT.JAVAHOUSE WHERE I DRANK GRANDE LATTES, DIGGING A MAD CAT FROM BAKERSFIELD.

WHAT KICKS!

KLIKKITY KLIK

LATER, IN A CHAT ROOM, I MET THE GONEST LITTLE GIRL AND HAD A WILD LOVE-FUELED EX-CHANGE, SHE WAS BEAUTIFUL AND SWEET AND SHE INTER-FACED LIKE AN ANGEL.

CRAZY!

KLIK KLIK

I NEEDED TO SPLIT, SO I WENT TO THE AOL LOBBY AND BEDDED DOWN WITH A CROWD OF SEARCH-ING PILGRIMS HUDDLED TO-GETHER IN A HUSHED DIGITAL GLOW.

ZZZ

A FEW HOURS LATER, I HOOKED UP WITH A CROWD OF FELLAS HEADING OVER TO A BLUES WEB SITE WHERE WE DOWNLOADED SOME CHOICE RIFFS AND REALLY WHOOPED IT UP.

WHOOO-EEE!

GO, GO, GO!

KLIK KLIK

EXHAUSTED, I ENDED MY FITFUL WANDERINGS, KNOWING I HAD DRANK DEEPLY FROM AMERICA'S CUP, HEARD ITS CRIES AND WHIS-PERS, AND HAD TRULY TRAVELED **AMERICA'S ROAD!**

NOW I'M READY TO BUY IT!

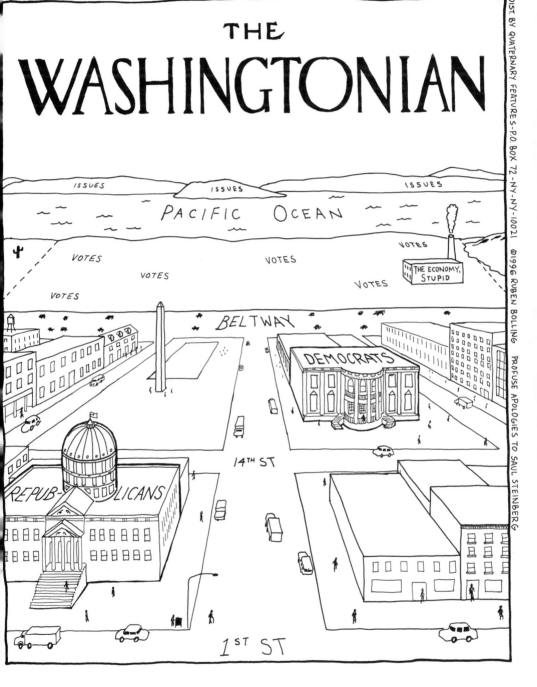

Tom the Dancing Bug

BY RUBEN BOLLING

TOMDBUG@AOL.COM

DIST. BY QUATERNARY FEATURES-P.O. BOX 72-NY-NY-10021 ©1996 R. BOLLING

HI, PERHAPS YOU'VE HEARD OF ME-- I'M **LYLE THE TALKING PIG.**

DID YOU KNOW THAT THE U.S. PIG POPULATION HAS DECLINED FROM ITS LEVEL OF 15 YEARS AGO?

THIS IS DIRECTLY ATTRIBUTABLE TO NEW HEALTH CONCERNS -- AMERICANS ARE **EATING** LESS OF US, SO THERE **ARE** LESS OF US.

PIGS AREN'T EXACTLY ENDANGERED, BUT OBVIOUSLY OUR **SUCCESS** AS A SPECIES DEPENDS ON OUR **USEFULNESS** TO HUMANS.

THAT'S WHY I'M ENDORSING THE XENOTRANSPLANT PROGRAM OF NERREX MEDICORP.

NERREX

GO AHEAD--YOU CAN EAT ALL THE TASTY PIG PRODUCTS YOU WANT!

PORK RINDS

THEN, WHEN YOUR HEART FINALLY GIVES OUT, WE NOW HAVE THE TECHNOLOGY TO HAVE A **PIG HEART** TRANSPLANTED.

NURSE! PORK-PUMP™ FROM NERREX, PLEASE!

THEN YOU CAN START ALL OVER!

YOU'LL BE HELPING THE PIG POPULATION-- AND EVEN ALLOWING PART OF ONE OF US TO LIVE ON, INSIDE YOU.

SO, HAVE A HEART--ONE OF OURS!

" MORE AND MORE-- YOU **ARE** WHAT YOU **EAT!** "

TOM the DANCING BUG

©1993 RUBEN BOLLING

SEX AND THE SINGLE AUSTRALO-PITHECINE

FEATURING CHARLEY, THE PREHISTORIC APE-MAN FROM THE PLIOCENE EPOCH. (AS IF YOU DIDN'T KNOW!)

AND SO CHARLEY WENT OUT ONE NIGHT IN SEARCH OF A MATE.

HEY, IT'S FRIDAY NIGHT!

AN AUSTRALOPITHECINE'S INSTINCTS CAN'T ALWAYS BE TRUSTED, AND CHARLEY WASTES TIME LOOKING FOR FEMALES AT A "WATERING HOLE".

I'LL JUST HANG AROUND A COUPLE MORE MINUTES...

HE EVENTUALLY FINDS HIS WAY TO A MORE APPROPRIATE VENUE.

I HOPE NONE OF THE FEMALES HERE HAVE GAZELLE-BREATH! I HATE THAT!

RECOGNIZING THAT A DISPLAY OF PHYSICAL PROWESS IS CALLED UPON, CHARLEY DOES HIS BEST TO IMPRESS.

THIS OUGHTA GET 'EM!

CHARLEY KNOWS THAT THE NEXT STEP IS DEMONSTRATING SOCIAL SKILLS.

SURE, YOU COULD ASK **WHY** MOVE "SAVED BY THE BELL" TO PRIME TIME. BUT **I** SAY: THEY'RE IN COLLEGE NOW. IT'S TIME!

MAYBE IF I IGNORE HIM...

AFTER A NUMBER OF FAILED ATTEMPTS, CHARLEY HOOKS UP WITH SOME OTHER ROGUE MALES.

ALL THE CHICKS HERE ARE TALL AND HAVE COMPLETELY **HAIRLESS FACES!**

BUT A FEW MORE OF THESE AND I WON'T MIND! **HAR!HAR!**

CHARLEY GETS A CRUCIAL TIP...

YOU'RE TRYING TOO HARD TOO FAST, MAN. YOUR GOAL SHOULD JUST BE TO GET *PHONE NUMBERS!*

...AND HE ENDS THE EVENING FEELING SUCCESSFUL-- AND YET VAGUELY UNFULFILLED.

I CAN'T BELIEVE THEY LEFT THIS LYING AROUND. IT'S A GOLD MINE!

WHITE PAGES

DIST. BY QUATERNARY FEATURES- P.O. BOX 72 -NY-NY-10021

BY RUBEN BOLLING

Now that Congress HAS FINALLY RECOGNIZED THE CRUSHING NEED AND BURNING DESIRE FOR THE **AMENDMENT** OF THE **CONSTITUTION** TO ALLOW **LAWS BANNING** THE **DESECRATION** OF THE AMERICAN **FLAG**, WE CAN EXPECT FOLLOWING **ADDITIONAL AMENDMENTS**, TRULY DESERVING TO BE PLACED BESIDE THE BILL OF RIGHTS AND THE EMANCIPATION PROCLAMATION AS PIECES OF TIMELESS WISDOM COMPRISING THE CORNERSTONE OF DEMOCRATIC PHILOSOPHY:

E-MAIL: TOMDBUG@AOL.COM — DIST. BY QUATERNARY FEATURES, P.O. BOX 72, NY, NY, 10021 — ©1995 R. BOLLING

Amendment XXIX: The Congress and the states shall have the power to prohibit the use of profanity in Patriotic Entertainment Parks.

OUR SOLDIERS DID NOT **SHED THEIR BLOOD** SO THAT SOME PUNK COULD FLIP THE BIRD AT A SOUVENIR CAMERA IN THE AMERICAN ADVENTURE PAVILION AT EPCOT CENTER!

Amendment XXX: The Congress and the states shall have the power to prohibit the use of U.S. currency in recreational or wagering contests.

SHALL WE HAVE BILLS BEARING THE LIKENESS OF OUR REVERED FIRST PRESIDENT **SULLIED** BY THE PLAYING OF "DOLLAR POKER" IN TAWDRY BARS?!!

Amendment XXXI: The Congress and the states shall have the power to prohibit the utterance of any modification of a patriotic song or pledge.

ALLOW ME TO READ FROM THE SHOCKING TRANSCRIPT OF A SONG OVERHEARD BEING SUNG BY A THIRD GRADER:

(AHEM) "THIS LAND IS MY LAND, THIS LAND AIN'T YOUR LAND, I'VE GOT A POP GUN, AND YOU DON'T GOT ONE."

Amendment XXXII: The Congress and the states shall have the power to prohibit the intentional misspelling of American military ranks for commercial purposes.

HOW MANY AMERICAN **CAPTAINS** HAVE TO LOSE THEIR LIVES DEFENDING OUR NATION BEFORE WE **BAN** ABOMINATIONS LIKE **THIS**?!

CAP'N CRUNCH

BY RUBEN BOLLING
EMAIL: TOMDBUG@AOL.COM

DIST. BY QUATERNARY FEATURES - PO BOX 72 - NY - NY - 10021

© 1995 R. BOLLING

THE ADVENTURES OF

SAM ROLAND

THE DETECTIVE WHO DIES

THE SECRET OF THE NITE CRAWLER CLUB

2:20 a.m. Stapleton is still in, and the lights are still on. The meeting is apparently continuing.

Where did it all begin? My client Chauncey Alcott put in a bid to buy the bankrupt "Nite Crawler" nightclub and received a threatening note.

ANY CLUES, MR. ROLAND?

HMM... UNSIGNED.

I decided to tail the previous owner, Snake Eyes "Mike" Stapleton, and found some suspicious goings-on.

WE MEET AT MIDNIGHT TO DISCUSS A "SITUATION."

I followed him here, and so I'm standing in a dark alley in a bad part of town in the wee hours of the..

GIVE ME YOUR MONEY.

WHAT?

GIVE ME YOUR MONEY *NOW!*

!

GET LOST! I'M BUS...

OOF

THE HAZARDS OF DETECTIVE WORK ARE NOT ALWAYS DIRECTLY RELATED TO THE INVESTIGATION, AND SO THE SECRET OF THE NITE CRAWLER CLUB SHALL ALWAYS REMAIN SUCH... AT LEAST TO *SAM ROLAND, THE DETECTIVE WHO DIES!*

NEWS of the TIMES

AILING DEATH ROW INMATE SEEKS RIGHT TO DIE

CHRISTOPHER MINTON, ON DEATH ROW FOR A CRIME HE DENIES TO HAVE COMMITTED, WAS RECENTLY DIAGNOSED WITH TERMINAL BRAIN CANCER. FACED WITH A CERTAIN AND PAINFUL DEATH, HE HAS REQUESTED A PHYSICIAN-ASSISTED SUICIDE, WHICH WAS DENIED BY THE STATE.

STATE SENATOR VERNON BELLUM:

WE WILL NOT ALLOW MINTON TO COMMIT SUICIDE--WE BELIEVE IN THE **SANCTITY** OF LIFE.

MINTON ALMOST COMPLI- CATED THE ISSUE WHEN HE RECENTLY ESCAPED FROM PRISON AND WAS CAPTURED JUST IN TIME...

WE'RE TAKING YOU BACK TO DEATH ROW!

EVEN IF MINTON WERE TO DROP THE APPEAL OF HIS CONVICTION, GOV. FRANCIS LANDERS STATES HE WOULD THEN RECONSIDER ALLOW- ING THE EXECUTION.

WE'D HAVE TO EXAMINE HIS MOTIVES TO BE SURE IT WASN'T A **TRICK** TO GET US TO KILL HIM.

IN FACT, AT A RECENT HEARING ON THAT APPEAL, STATE LAWYERS VOICED SUCH SUSPICIONS TO THE COURT.

YOUR HONOR, MINTON'S COUNSEL ISN'T EVEN **TRYING**! THEY **CLEARLY** SHOULD HAVE OBJECTED TO MY LAST STATEMENT!

A **LAW-ABIDING CITIZEN** CAN'T GET AN ASSISTED SUICIDE--WHY SHOULD A **CONVICTED FELON**?!

I'M SICK OF THE STATE **CODDLING** PRISONERS WITH EXTRA ADVANTAGES LIKE GIVING 'EM FREE CABLE T.V., AND KILLING 'EM AND SUCH.

TOM THE DANCING BUG

©1992 RUBEN BOLLING

DIST. BY QUATERNARY FEATURES · P.O. BOX 72 · NY · NY · 10021

"TOM THE DANCING BUG"

Games Louis Plays.

BY RUBEN BOLLING

TOMDBUG@AOL.COM

DIST. BY QUATERNARY FEATURES - P.O. BOX 72 - NY-NY-10021 ©1996 R. BOLLING

Panel 1:

MOM, DO WE HAVE ANY BOOKS ON THE OLYMPICS?

UM...THERE'S SOME INFORMATION IN THE ALMANAC IN THE DEN.

Panel 2:

HERE COMES THE BIG MOMENT IN THE TRACK AND FIELD EVENTS.

YOUNG LOUIS MALTBY IS WARMING UP TO COMPETE FOR THE GOLD!

Panel 3:

BY NOW, YOU ALL KNOW THE INCREDIBLE STORY OF MALTBY-- ONLY A FEW MONTHS AGO, HE WAS THE WORST ATHLETE IN HIS ENTIRE ELEMENTARY SCHOOL CLASS.

Panel 4:

THEN, ON FEBRUARY 9, IN GYM CLASS, THERE WAS A **CRAB-WALK RACE**, AND MALTBY CAME IN **FIRST**--THE ONLY RACE HE'D **EVER** WON!

REENACTMENT

Panel 5:

THAT WAS WHEN LOUIS MALTBY'S LIFE CHANGED--IT WAS DISCOVERED THAT HE HAD A MIRACULOUS GIFT FOR CRAB-WALKING!

Maltby Breaks State Crab-Walking Record

Sets mark after winning fateful Gym-Class Race

Panel 6:

MALTBY WAS THRUST INTO THE INTERNATIONAL CRAB-WALKING CIRCUIT, AND NOW, DESPITE HIS YOUTH, HE IS FAVORED TO WIN IT ALL.

Panel 7:

THE CRAB-WALKERS ARE TAKING THEIR POSITIONS-- HERE IS THE MOMENT OF TRUTH FOR MALTBY AND U.S.A.

Panel 8:

MOM, IF A CERTAIN KIND OF RACE ISN'T LISTED IN THE ALMANAC, DOES THAT MEAN IT'S NOT AN OLYMPIC EVENT?

I WOULD THINK SO, LOUIS. WHY?

Panel 9:

NOTHING. OH, I WON A CRAB-WALK RACE IN GYM TODAY.

THAT'S NICE.

TOM the DANCING BUG

BY RUBEN BOLLING
TOMDBUG@AOL.COM

Those CUTE CANADIANS!

OUR ADORABLE NEIGHBORS TO THE NORTH ARE HAVING A SQUABBLE!

YOU SEE, MOST CANADIANS TALK JUST LIKE US, ONLY MORE MID-WESTERN-LIKE.

HOW ABOOT SOME MORE SYRUP, EH?

ALRIGHTY.

Did you Know? DURING CANADA'S SUMMER MONTHS, SOME OF ITS LANDSCAPE IS NOT COVERED IN SNOW!

BUT PART OF CANADA, CALLED QUEBEC, HAS THREATENED TO SECEDE! WHY? BECAUSE THEY LIKE TO SPEAK FRENCH!

ZIS EES ZE WAY I PARLEZ, MONSIEUR!

YOU CANNOT STOP ME!

Did you Know? CANADA ACTUALLY HAS ITS OWN GOVERNMENT!

ISN'T THAT PRECIOUS?! APPARENTLY THEY NOT ONLY LIKE TO SPEAK LIKE EUROPEANS, THEY'RE ALSO JUST AS TOUCHY!

OKAY, OKAY! YOU CAN SPEAK FRENCH!

NON! EES NOT GOOD ENOUGH! AU REVOIR!

Did you Know? BEFORE ALAN THICKE AND MICHAEL J. FOX BECAME HOLLYWOOD STARS, THEY WERE FROM CANADA!

INSTEAD OF AN EPIC CIVIL WAR OVER THE SECESSION, THEY HAD A VOTE!

ALRIGHT! OUI! WE STAY! BUT WE'RE STEEL MAD!

50.6 % NON

Did you Know? THE F.A.A. DEEMS FLIGHTS BETWEEN CANADA AND THE U.S. AS "INTERNATIONAL"!

HA-HA! WHAT A POLITICAL STORM! IT'S LIKE THEY HAVE THEIR OWN COUNTRY UP THERE!

ALRIGHT! BREAK IT UP!

OO! LOOK, A MOUNTIE! THEY'RE THE CUTEST!

Did you Know? 73% OF AMERICANS THINK CANADA SHOULD BE ALLOWED TO BECOME THE 51ST STATE!

Tom the Dancing Bug

BY RUBEN BOLLING

ONE STORMY NIGHT ON THE DUDE RANCH.

LOOKS LIKE IT'S GONNA RAIN BUT HARD!

YEP.

HEY, LISTEN! DO YOU HEAR THAT? SOUNDS LIKE A...

RUMBLE RUMBLE RUMBLE

STAMPEDE!!

DIST. BY QUATERNARY FEATURES - P.O. BOX 72 - N.Y., N.Y. 10021 - ©1994 RUBEN BOLLING - EMAIL: TOMDBUG @ AOL.COM

SLIM, YOU AND TAYLOR RIDE TO THE HEAD OF THE HERD AND STEER IT AROUND! WE'LL MEET YOU AT THE BLUFF!

THEY'RE HEADIN' TOWARD THE RIVER! MOVE!!

DUDE!

DUDE!

DUDE!

HATE

WHEW! WE FINALLY GOT THESE DUDES UNDER CONTROL!

DUDE!

DUDE

DUDE!

RECKON THERE'S NO WAY TO KNOW WHAT STARTED THAT...

I FOUND THE CULPRIT ON A TREE BACK YONDER.

A FLYER FOR A PEARL JAM CONCERT IN TOWN!

DAGNABBIT! I'M GETTIN' TOO OLD FER THIS WORK...

DUDE!

THANX TO THE MERTZES!

©1992 RUBEN BOLLING

Under the Clean Air Act, companies can emit up to a certain level of pollutants. But a company that emits **less** than that level can **sell** its unused portion to another company whose emissions **exceed** that level.

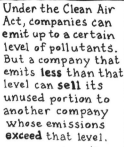

WHERE WILL THIS LEAD...?

TALES OF MARKET-DRIVEN CRIMES

MARTIN RYDER IS AWAKENED BY THE SOUNDS OF A BURGLARY.

HIS HAND REACHES TO A DRAWER...

AND HE CORNERS THE SURPRISED INTRUDER!

I HAVE EVERY RIGHT TO KILL YOU-- I'M IN MY OWN DWELLING, AND I FEAR FOR MY OWN LIFE!

BUT I HAVE A BETTER IDEA!

HELLO, CRIME-BROKERS? I HAVE A JUSTIFIABLE HOMICIDE I'D LIKE TO SELL.

CERTAINLY, SIR. THE GOING RATE FOR THE RIGHT TO KILL IS $30,000.

CRIME BROK...

DONE!

MOMENTS LATER...

YEH? YOU FOUND A SELLER? THANKS, CRIME-BROKERS.

OKAY, SLUGGO. GO AHEAD.

RYDER DECIDED NOT TO USE HIS LEGAL RIGHT TO KILL, BUT INSTEAD SOLD IT TO SLUGGO WHO HAD NO SUCH RIGHT. THUS, RYDER OVERCOMPLIED WITH THE LAW SO THAT SLUGGO COULD UNDERCOMPLY.

OKAY, BUB, BEAT IT! SCOOT!

THE SAME NUMBER OF DEATHS RESULT, BUT WITH A MORE EFFICIENT ALLOCATION.

ANOTHER HAPPY OUTCOME, WHEN CRIMES ARE MARKET-DRIVEN!

QUATERNARY FEATURES-P.O. BOX 72 - NY-NY-10021

Tom the Dancing Bug
BY ©Ruben Bolling

HARVEY RICHARDS

AMERICA'S FOREMOST AUTHORITY ON **CHILDREN'S LAW** PRESENTS HIS NEW BOOK...

RICHARDS ON SIBLINGS

HARVEY RICHARDS, ESQ. "LAWYER FOR CHILDREN"

MR. RICHARDS SAYS:

THE FIERCEST BATTLES IN THE CHILDREN'S LAW ARENA ARE FOUGHT IN THE FIELD OF SIBLING LAW!

MY BOOK WILL SHOW YOU HOW TO ASSERT YOUR RIGHTS IN THIS HIGHLY-CHARGED AREA!

FOR EXAMPLE, THERE'S AN ENTIRE CHAPTER ON T.V. CHANNEL LAWS.

CAN'T TURN IN THE MIDDLE OF A SHOW!!

AH, BUT I DEFINE A "SHOW" AS EACH INDIVIDUAL SESAME STREET SKETCH, AND THE GROVER SKETCH IS OVER!

MOST CHILDREN DON'T NEED ADVICE ON WHEN TO APPEAL TO PARENTAL AUTHORITY...

I'M TELLING!

... BUT MANY CAN USE EXPERT TIPS ON DEALING WITH THAT AUTHORITY, SUCH AS KEEPING ACCURATE AND DETAILED RECORDS.

MARCH 4, 1990: WHEN JUDY WAS THREE MONTHS YOUNGER THAN I AM NOW, *SHE* WAS ALLOWED TO STAY UP PAST 9:00 ON A SCHOOLNIGHT!

AND, OF COURSE, DETAILED TREATMENT OF *BACKSEAT TERRITORY LAW*:

p.317: IN ORDER TO PROPERLY ASSERT YOUR RIGHTS, YOU MUST CONSTANTLY USE EVERY INCH OF YOUR ENTITLEMENT.

p.348: THE THREE-SIBLING APPROACH TO THE CAR: WHO WILL HAVE TO SIT IN THE MIDDLE?

Note the disadvantage of A, who approached the car first. He runs the risk of a "run-around maneuver" by B.

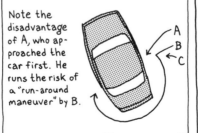

DO YOU WANT TO LIVE THE REST OF YOUR LIFE IN YOUR SIBLING'S **SHADOW?!** YOU CAN *WIN* SIBLING RIVALRY! BUY THIS BOOK **TODAY!**

PRESENTS:

NEWS of THE TIMES

TOMDBUG@AOL.COM

FRESHMAN
CONGRESSMAN:
"PLENTY
OF TIME
UNTIL
21ST CENTURY!"

FRESHMAN REPRESENTATIVE GORDON FORRESTER (D.Cal.) HAS CHARACTERIZED PRESIDENT CLINTON'S PLAN TO PREPARE FOR THE 21ST CENTURY AS "OVERZEALOUS" AND "DWEEBY."

I HAVE NO ISSUE WITH THE SUBSTANCE OF HIS PLAN--JUST THE **TIMING**...

I MEAN, WE'VE GOT LIKE **THREE YEARS** TO GET THAT DONE. WHAT KIND OF **GEEK** STARTS **THAT** LONG BEFORE A DEADLINE?

INTERVIEWED AT HIS GEORGETOWN RESIDENCE, FORRESTER EXPLAINED HIS POSITION AND SHOWED OFF HIS NEW "BITCHIN'" STEREO SYSTEM.

BACK IN STATE SENATE, I WROTE A WHOLE BILL ON GRAZING LANDS BY PULLING AN ALL-NIGHTER.

DOWN THE HALL, OTHER FRESHMEN WERE FOUND TO SUPPORT FORRESTER.

I USED TO THINK CLINTON WAS COOL-- YOU KNOW, HIS SUCCESS WITH THE LADIES. BUT NOW FORRESTER IS MUCH COOLER. I SAY WE **PARTY UNTIL 1999**!!

WOOO!

HOWEVER, FORRESTER HAS NOT BEEN AS POPULAR WITH MORE SENIOR CONGRESSMEN, WHO HAVE LET HIM KNOW IN SUBTLE WAYS.

HEY!

OH, SORRY.

CLINTON HIMSELF HAS TAKEN ON THE FORRESTER FACTION.

THESE FRESHMEN THINK THEY CAN **PROCRASTINATE** AND THEN DO A RUSHED JOB...

BUT THIS "BRIDGE TO THE 21ST CENTURY" IS **MY** PROJECT--AND HISTORY IS GRADING **ME**!

TOM THE DANCING BUG

©1993 RUBEN BOLLING

THE OUTER REACHES OF PLOT TWISTS

PEOPLE! BAH! WHO NEEDS THEM?! I WISH THERE WERE *NO OTHER PEOPLE!*

SUBMITTED FOR YOUR APPROVAL: JONATHAN P. MASON. WOULD-BE HERMIT AND GENERALLY CRANKY PERSON.

HE WILL GET HIS WISH OF ANCHORITISM, BUT WILL ALSO GET NOT ONE, BUT **SEVERAL** BITTERLY IRONIC **PLOT TWISTS!**

THE NEXT MORNING...

I DON'T BELIEVE IT!

THEY'RE ALL GONE! I'M ALL ALONE!!

BUT... WHAT'S THAT NOISE?

RUMBLE

GIANT WOMBATS!

I WISHED THERE WERE NO PEOPLE, BUT I **DIDN'T** WISH THERE WOULDN'T BE **GIANT WOMBATS!** WHAT A **SURPRISING TWIST!**

BUT WAIT! I FORGOT! I AM A **MARSUPIOLOGIST!** THIS IS AN EXCELLENT OPPORTUNITY TO STUDY THESE ANIMALS!!

HOW IRONIC!

AND I W... AAAA

SPLAT!

JONATHAN P. MASON. HE WAS GRANTED HIS SOLITUDE, BUT THE TOTALLY UNEXPECTED PLOT TWISTS WERE A BIT MORE THAN THE MISANTHROPIC MARSUPIOLOGIST HAD BARGAINED FOR.

ALSO, HE WAS A MARTIAN.

DIST. BY QUATERNARY FEATURES-P.O. BOX 72-NY-NY-10021

55

TOM the DANCING BUG

BY RUBEN BOLLING
DIST. BY QUATERNARY FEATURES
PO BOX 72-NY-NY 10021

WRITER/DIRECTOR/ACTOR BRIAN WASS ON HIS NEW FILM:

"EVERYONE TALKS ABOUT **GENERATION X** LIKE IT'S THIS LOST GENERATION. MAN, THEY'VE BEEN MASS-MARKETED AND PANDERED TO AT A YOUNGER AGE THAN ANY GENERATION IN HISTORY."

"AND THE **BABY BOOMERS**? FORGET IT! THEY HAVE THEIR MONOLITHIC CULTURAL ICONS-- WOODSTOCK, THE BIG CHILL, 'NAM...'"

"WHAT ABOUT PEOPLE LIKE ME? BORN IN THE **EARLY** SIXTIES, MAN, **WE'RE** THE LOST GENERATION-- BETWEEN THE YUPPIES AND THE SLACKERS. I CALL MY FILM **'WEDGIES'** BECAUSE WE'RE WEDGED BETWEEN THESE TWO HUGE PHENOMENONS."

FROM "WEDGIES":

I CAN'T BELIEVE HE BROKE UP WITH ME! GOD, I FEEL LIKE BRENDA MORGENSTERN!

THEN I'LL BE RHODA... LET'S GET THE SARA LEE OUT OF THE FREEZER.

"SO MANY FILMS TRY SO HARD TO SPEAK FOR A GENERATION. WEDGIES REJECT THAT MENTALITY. WE HAVE A POSTMODERN OUTLOOK THAT RECOGNIZES AND SCOFFS AT DEMOGRAPHIC HUCKSTERISM."

♪ EVERYBODY WAS KUNG FU FIGHTING! THOSE CATS WERE FAST AS LIGHTNING! ♪

OH, I LOVE THIS SONG!

WOW. I SURE COULD GO FOR SOME POP ROCKS.

"YOU HAVE TO BE **REAL**. YOU CAN'T COMMODIFY THE WEDGIE'S CULTURE, BECAUSE THEY'LL SEE RIGHT THROUGH YOU."

I'M GOING TO SHOP-RITE. WHAT DO WE NEED?

UM... SOME DIET PEPSI, FIG NEWTONS, AND A SIX OF NEW ICE LITE FROM MILLER. "MORE OF WHAT YOU WANT, LESS OF WHAT YOU DON'T."

DO YOU SEE YOURSELF AS A SPOKESMAN FOR YOUR GENERATION?

"FRANKLY, I'D RATHER BE A SPOKESMODEL-- I'D GET TO MEET ED McMAHON.

...SEE? I'M IRONICALLY DISAFFECTED."

© 1994 RUBEN BOLLING

Games Louis Plays.

THE BALL'S **NEVER** HIT OUT HERE...

DIST BY QUATERNARY CREATURES · P.O. BOX 72 · NY · NY · 10021 · ©1994 RUBEN BOLLING

BUT I'LL SHOW THEM! I'LL BE CONSTANTLY READY!

More Thoughts of a Rightfielder.

AND IF THE BALL **IS** HIT HERE, I'LL REACH UP AND MAKE A GREAT CATCH!

AND THEN LATER, I'LL MAKE A CATCH SPRINTING TO MY RIGHT! THE CROWD GOES WILD!

NO, WAIT! I'LL CATCH IT RUNNING BACK, OVER MY SHOULDER, LIKE THIS!

THUNK

...AND THEN WHIRL AROUND AND HURL THE BALL BACK IN!

IF YOU'RE DONE WITH YOUR DANCE, YOU CAN THROW THE BALL IN, LOUIS. THE BASES ARE CLEARED!

AND THEN, WHEN I BAT...

57

TOM the Dancing Bug

©1993 RUBEN BOLLING

DIST. BY QUATERNARY FEATURES—PO BOX 72-NY-NY-10021

AND SO, YOUR HONOR, MY CLIENT WISHES TO **SEVER** ALL TIES TO HER **BIOLOGICAL PARENTS.**

ON WHAT GROUNDS?

SHE HAS TO DO MORE CHORES BUT GETS LESS ALLOWANCE THAN **ANY OF HER FRIENDS!** I HAVE SIGNED AFFIDAVITS FROM 12 CLASSMATES.

SHE IS FREQUENTLY SERVED ICKY FOODS FOR DINNER, AND HER TV PRIVILEGES ARE OPPRESSIVELY LIMITED TO PUBLIC TELEVISION AND EDUCATIONAL VIDEOS!

THAT'S RIDICULOUS! WITH WHOM WOULD SHE BE LIVING?!

WE PROPOSE THAT SHE LIVE IN THE PLAYHOUSE IN THE BACKYARD. HER MOTHER COULD BRING OUT HER MEALS...

COUNSELOR, APPROACH THE BENCH.

MR. RICHARDS, WHAT IS GOING ON HERE?! WHO DO YOU THINK YOU ARE?!!

I'M **HARVEY RICHARDS, LAWYER FOR CHILDREN!**

BECAUSE OF RECENT PRECEDENTS, I'M BRANCHING OUT INTO COURTROOM PRACTICE.

THIS IS THE MOST **IMPROPER, INCOMPETENT AND IRRESPONSIBLE** SUIT I'VE EVER SEEN A LAWYER BRING!

WELL, I'M **RUBBER,** YOU'RE **GLUE!** IT BOUNCES OFF **ME** AND STICKS TO **YOU!**

...AND THEN HE DISMISSED THE CASE AND FINED ME FOR **CONTEMPT OF COURT!** I CAN'T BELIEVE A JUDGE COULD BE SO UNKNOWLEDGEABLE ABOUT BASIC LEGAL PRINCIPLES!

 **TOM the DANCING BUG**

BY RUBEN BOLLING

EMAIL: TOMBUG@AOL.COM

THE ADVENTURES OF

SAM ROLAND

THE DETECTIVE WHO DIES

THE CASE OF THE JUPITER DIAMOND

UNDER NIGHT'S BLANKET OF DARKNESS, A LONE FIGURE MAKES ITS IMPROBABLE WAY UP THE SIDE OF A LUXURY HI-RISE.

GLASS IS SOUNDLESSLY CUT...

...AND SOPHISTICATED SECURITY DEVICES ARE METHODICALLY ELUDED.

EXPERT FINGERS FEEL THEIR WAY PAST A COMBINATION LOCK...

...AND DAZZLING BRILLIANCE IS REVEALED!

RRRING! RRRING!

HELLO?

WHAT?! THE JUPITER DIAMOND **STOLEN?!**

DIST. BY QUATERNARY FEATURES · P.O. BOX 72 · N·Y·N·Y· 10021

I'D BETTER **HURRY!** THIS MAY BE THE MOST IMPORTANT CASE OF MY CAREER!

WHA?

BONK!

UGH!

IN THE PURSUIT OF TRUTH AND JUSTICE, A DETECTIVE MUST RISK HIS LIFE IN MANY WAYS. **75%** OF ALL ACCIDENTS OCCUR IN THE **BATHROOM,** AND **THAT** IS WHERE UNDUE HASTE ENDS THE CASE OF THE JUPITER DIAMOND—AT LEAST FOR **SAM ROLAND, THE DETECTIVE WHO DIES!**

The Wit & Wisdom of
Charley the
Australopithecine

LIFE IS LIKE A BOX OF CHOCOLATES...

LEAVE ME ALONE.

IT'S OVER-PRICED AND MOST THINGS IN IT SUCK.

I'M WARNIN' YOU--STOP TALKIN' TO ME.

"I WAS KIND OF AN UN-USUAL CHILD..."

LOOK, PEGGY! I KILLED THIS SQUIRREL JUST FOR YOU!

CHARLEY, YOU ARE DISGUSTIN'!

"BUT MY TALENT FOR BRACHI-ATING GOT ME ON THE GYM-NASTICS TEAM."

I'M GONNA MAKE YOU A STAR!

COACH

"WHEN THE TEAM WON THE NATIONAL CHAMP-IONSHIP, I MET THAT PRESIDENT KENNEDY-- WHAT A NICE FELLA!"

HEY, HOW COME YOU GET TWO AND I ONLY GET ONE?!

BECAUSE I'M THE PRESIDENT, CHAHLEY.

"SEE, I'M A THROWBACK TO A SIM-PLER TIME, SO I DON'T TAKE TO MODERN STUFF."

BOY, ARE YOU *STUPID!*

LIMITED CRANIAL CAPACITY *IS* AS LIMITED CRANIAL CAPACITY *DOES!*

"OF COURSE, I SOON BECAME A MILLIONAIRE BECAUSE IN AMERICA, ANYONE WHO'S SWEET AND GOOD-NATURED MAKES LOADS OF DOUGH."

Fortune FEB.1986

PRE-HISTORIC APE-MAN HITS IT BIG IN JUNK BONDS

YEP. A BOX OF CHOCOLATES IS JUST **LIKE** LIFE -- CAUSES ZITS.

WHAT'S A BLAST OF **MACE** LIKE?

DIST. BY QUATERNARY FEATURES-P.O. BOX 72 -NY-NY-10021 - ©1994 RUBEN BOLLING - EMAIL: TOMDBUG@AOL.COM

by RUBEN BOLLING
tomdbug@aol.com

DIST. BY QUATERNARY FEATURES ©1996 R. BOLLING

NEWS of the TIMES

ALIENS REVEAL THEMSELVES AND EXPLAIN PURPOSE

AT AN APOLOGETIC PRESS CONFERENCE, TWO SPOKES-ALIENS EXPRESSED REGRET ABOUT THEIR HERETOFORE CLANDESTINE ACTIVITIES ON EARTH.

WE ARE NOT HERE TO INVADE, SUBJUGATE OR EVEN STUDY HUMANS. OUR PLANS ARE SIMPLY TO...

...INTRODUCE YOU TO AN *EXCITING NEW DELICIOUS SNACK FOOD--* **MEATLOAF-ON-A-STICK™!**

Meatloaf-On-A-Stick™

"WE REGRET THE OCCASIONAL ABDUCTION OF HUMANS, BUT IT WAS NECESSARY FOR OUR FOCUS GROUPS."

"WE WOULD SIMPLY FEED OUR GUESTS NUTRITIOUS MEATLOAF-BASED SNACKS..."

WHAT DO YOU THINK? TOO MUCH PARSLEY?

"...AND SEND THEM ON THEIR WAY, WITH MEMORIES ERASED AND, AMAZINGLY, *NO TIME ELAPSED!*"

"YES, THAT'S THE KEY TO OUR FAST-FOOD CONCEPT--WE'LL USE OUR SUPER-TECHNOLOGY TO EASE THE STRESS OF TODAY'S EARTHLING'S BUSY LIFESTYLE!"

MEMORY ERASURE CAN BE TRICKY, THOUGH, AND SOME TEST-CUSTOMERS HAVE BEEN LEFT WITH CERTAIN DELUSIONAL IMPRINTS.

THAT'S WHY WE MAKE THIS PLEDGE:

IT IS NOT *Meatloaf-On-A-Stick*™'s POLICY TO TORMENT, CROSS-SPECIES BREED WITH, OR PROBE ANY ORIFICE OF, OUR VALUED CUSTOMERS.

THE ENTREPENEURIAL ALIENS ALSO DENIED ANY INVOLVEMENT WITH UNEXPLAINED COW MUTILATIONS.

WE USE ONLY LEGALLY PURCHASED GRADE "A" CHUCK!

THAT'S PROBABLY THOSE GUYS FROM PLANET ZOREK. THEY'RE HERE TEST-MARKETING "BOVINE-ENTRAILS-IN-A-CUP" FRANCHISES.

Louis's Guide To Writing Book Reports Without Reading Books.

① WHEN THE TEACHER REMINDS THE CLASS THAT THE REPORT IS DUE TOMORROW, IT'S TIME TO START.

OH YEAH...

② GO TO THE LIBRARY AND CHOOSE A GOOD BOOK -- WITH LOTS OF PICTURES.

③ READ THE INSIDE COVER AND BACK COVER VERY CAREFULLY. LOOK AT THE PICTURES.

④ BE SURE NOT TO USE THE EXACT WORDS FROM THESE COVERS. TEACHERS CAN TELL WHEN SOMETHING WASN'T WRITTEN BY A 4TH-GRADER.

This book spans the thrilling life of American frontiersman Davy Crockett. From the opening chapter, in which a young Crockett must wrestle a mighty grizzly,

⑤ DID YOU LIKE THE BOOK? YOU <u>LOVED</u> IT!

<u>Davy Crockett, Wilderness Hero</u>, by Samuel Mitchell was my favorite book I ever read. It was really good when he fought a bear. But the whole book was excellent. It was very exciting and

⑥ AFTER YOU'VE GAINED CONFIDENCE, YOU CAN SIMPLIFY THE PROCESS AND DO REPORTS ON BOOKS THAT DON'T EVEN EXIST.

<u>Sulu's Ghost</u>, by Darryl Canseco, Jr. This was an excellent book about Star Trek. Mr. Sulu dies and he haunts the Enterprise. First, Captain Kirk thinks its a bad ghost,

TOM THE DANCING BUG

BY RUBEN BOLLING

DIST. BY QUATERNARY FEATURES · P.O. BOX 72 · NY-NY-10021 · ©1995 R. BOLLING · eMAIL · TOMDBUG@AOL.COM

I'M AN UNWED PREGNANT WOMAN, AND I JUST DON'T KNOW WHAT TO DO!

I WISH OUR POLITICAL LEADERS WOULD PROVIDE MARKET-BASED INCENTIVES TO HELP ME MAKE THE *RIGHT CHOICE!*

HERE YOU GO, LITTLE LADY! $3,000 TO FORGO THE ABORTION AND PUT YOUR BABY UP FOR ADOPTION!

OH MY!

YES, WE NOW KNOW THAT THE ONLY WAY TO CORRECT BEHAVIOR IS THROUGH *COLD CASH!*

WITH PROGRAMS LIKE THIS PROPOSED UTAH PLAN FOR UNWED MOTHERS-TO-BE, AND GINGRICH'S "EARNING BY LEARNING" PROGRAM...

SIR, I FINISHED READING "THE FOUNTAINHEAD"

HERE YA GO, KID.

...WE CAN HARNESS MARKET FORCES TO MAKE AMERICA *OUR* KIND OF PLACE!

EVERYBODY WINS WHEN WE IMPROVE OUR COUNTRY BY OFFERING PROPER INCENTIVES TO--

HOMOSEXUALS...

I GET 50 BUCKS EACH TIME I SLEEP WITH A WOMAN!

LIBERALS...

I GET $10 EVERY TIME I DENOUNCE MY MAMBY-PAMBY, OUTDATED POLITICAL PHILOSOPHY.

KA-CHING!

HERE YOU ARE!

MINORITIES

I GET PAID $100 A DAY JUST FOR STAYING OUT OF SIGHT!

US MAIL

MARKET-DRIVEN MOTIVATION: MOLDING AMERICA THROUGH THE **RIGHT** INCENTIVES!

"TOM the DANCING BUG"
THE LOONEY TOONIFICATION OF AMERICA
BY RUBEN BOLLING

YES, VIOLENCE IN AMERICA HAS TAKEN ON A CARTOON QUALITY. THE COUNTRY FINDS ITS AMUSEMENT IN SIMPLE, REPETITIVE TALES OF AGGRESSION AND REVENGE, ALL DIGESTED DOWN TO SEVEN-MINUTE INFOTAINMENT SEGMENTS. OUR FAVORITE "NEWS" CHARACTERS PERFORM ACTS OF AGGRESSION WITH AS MUCH DRAMATIC AND COMIC FLAIR (AND WITH ABOUT AS MUCH IMPUNITY) AS THEIR ANIMATED COUNTERPARTS EVER DID.

64

TOM the DANCING BUG

TOM the DANCING BUG

©1992 *Ruben Bolling*

DIST. BY QUATERNARY FEATURES · P.O. BOX 72 · NY · NY · NY · 10021

FASTEN YOUR SEATBELTS! IT'S A

SATURDAY
with **BOB**

ACTION · ADVENTURE · THRILLS · CHILLS

BOB RISES AT 9:42, HIS HEAD STILL WOOZY FROM THE PREVIOUS NIGHT'S OVER-INDULGENCE IN CHICKEN WINGS AND BEN & JERRY'S!

THE ENJOYMENT OF HIS SHOW-ER IS MARRED--THE SOAP IS A MERE SLIVER, AND THE LAST DROPS OF SHAMPOO MUST BE COAXED FROM THE CONTAINER!

BOB BOLDLY SHAKES OFF HIS RAGE, AND WITH A BELLY-FUL OF CINNAMON LIFE CEREAL, HE IS READY TO FACE THE CHAL-LENGES OF THE NEW DAY!

DESPITE BOB'S CAREFUL CALCULATIONS, SHOPPING FOR MORE BATHROOM SUPPLIES ALWAYS TAKES MORE TIME THAN ANTICIPATED!

IT'S LUNCH-TIME, AND BOB HAS BEEN HANKERING FOR SOME DINTY MOORE BEEF STEW! FROM CAN TO MICROWAVE TO STOMACH, BOB IS SATED IN LESS THAN TWENTY MINUTES!

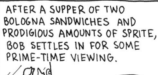

COLLEGE FOOTBALL HOLDS BOB'S RAPT ATTENTION FOR MUCH OF THE AFTERNOON, ASIDE FROM A FEW DEFTLY EXECUTED FORAYS INTO CABLE'S UPPER REACHES DURING COMMERCIALS.

AFTER A SUPPER OF TWO BOLOGNA SANDWICHES AND PRODIGIOUS AMOUNTS OF SPRITE, BOB SETTLES IN FOR SOME PRIME-TIME VIEWING.

LATER, BOB'S PRACTICED EYE WILL ENDEAVOR TO DECIPHER THE SCRAMBLED IMAGES OF THE PLAYBOY CHANNEL. THEN BOB WILL COLLAPSE INTO BED, EX-HAUSTED BUT READY FOR WHAT-EVER ADVENTURES SUNDAY MIGHT BRING.

TOM THE DANCING BUG

©1993 Ruben Bolling

DESPERATE FOR FUNDING AFTER THE FAILURE OF **BIOSPHERE 2**, SPACE BIOSPHERE VENTURES FORMS AN ALLIANCE WITH A CABLE NETWORK FOR ITS NEXT PROJECT...

MTV's REAL WORLD BIOSPHERE

WITH THE VIDEO CAMERAS CONSTANTLY RUNNING, THIS IS THE CHRONICLE OF A DIVERSE GROUP OF YOUNG, TELEGENIC PSEUDOSCIENTISTS HANGING OUT FOR A SUMMER IN A **SELF-CONTAINED BEACH HOUSE** IN BELMAR, N.J.

SEE, THE PROBLEM WITH BIOSPHERE 2 WAS THAT THEY WERE WAY TOO DORKY.

EXCEPT THE BALD GUY. HE WAS COOL.

THIS EXPERIMENT IS, LIKE, REALLY... BOLD, YOU KNOW?

ASH LANGSTON
SPECIALIST: INTERPERSONAL VIBES

HEY, YOU WANT PEPPERONI ON IT?

GORDON, YOUR BURRITO SPLATTERED ALL OVER THE MICROWAVE AGAIN!

AH, YOU'RE JUST PISSED 'CAUSE YOU BLEW THAT DORITOS COMMERCIAL AUDITION.

YO, MAN! THEY CALL THIS **SELF-CONTAINED?!** WE'RE ALREADY OUT OF SNAPPLE!

THEN HAVE A BREW, DUDE.

YOU GUYS ARE GOING TO USE MY NICKNAME, **DINGO**, RIGHT? DON'T USE MY REAL NAME...

SETH HURWITZ
SPECIALIST: C.D. CLUB MEMBERSHIP MANAGEMENT

MAN, I AM **SO** HUNGOVER.

HUH, HUH. HUH, HUH.

I'M HEADIN' OUT TO THE 7-11 ECOSYSTEM. ANYONE WANT ANYTHING?

THE EXPERIMENT CONTINUES!

DIST. BY QUATERNARY FEATURES. P.O. BOX 72, N.Y. NY. 10021

Tom the Dancing Bug

©1992 Ruben Bolling

The "**S**ecret, **W**holly **I**nsidious **S**ociety of **H**omosexuals" will now come to order.

First, we'll hear from our director of **Media Manipulation**.

By the way, great disguise.

Thanks. They never suspect!

S.W.I.S.H.

I am pleased to announce that our **infiltration** of the media is now **complete!**

Despite our obviously depraved lifestyle, fully **3%** of all T.V. and movie homosexuals are portrayed in a positive light!

Clap! Clap!

Well done!

Clap! Clap!

Divine!

Clap! Clap!

Now we'll hear from our director of **Unbridled Legislative Power**.

Thank you.

S.W.I.S.H.

Things could not be better. We have all kinds of **rights** and **entitlements** that heterosexuals only dream of!

For example, only **24** out of 50 states have statutes that outlaw our very existence.

Wow!

Un-believ-able!

Well, we've got 'em where we want 'em! Now we'll hear from...

Clap! Clap!

Clap! Clap!

WHOOP! WHOOP!

WHOOP! OOP! OOP! WH

Code **Lavender** alarm! Where is the situation?!

Bakersfield Mall, sir. A man is holding his wife's **purse** while she tries on clothes...

Finley! Garcia! Get over there, quick! He's in a weakened state! He can be **converted!!**

S.W.

Ha! Ha! Silly heterosexuals! If they continue to ignore their conservative leaders, we'll soon take over **the country!**

DIST. BY QUATERNARY FEATURES—P.O. BOX 72-NY-NY-10021

Tom the Dancing Bug

©1993 Ruben Bolling

HELLO. YOU MAY KNOW ME AS HARVEY RICHARDS: LAWYER FOR CHILDREN.

I'VE DEVOTED MY LEGAL CAREER TO INTERPRETING AND ENFORCING **CHILDREN'S** LEGAL CODES.

BUT DID YOU KNOW THAT I ALSO HANDLE CERTAIN **ADULT** CASES?-- PROVIDING THE ADULTS INVOLVED ARE SUFFICIENTLY **IMMATURE!**

MANY ADULTS STILL ABIDE BY CHILDLIKE RULES LIKE THOSE OF THEIR PAST! THESE RULES CAN BE APPLIED IN NUMEROUS SITUATIONS...

SEATING RULES...

HEY! **I** WAS SITTING THERE!

"SHUFFLE YOUR MEAT, LOSE YOUR SEAT"!

BEER PITCHER RULES...

"YOU KILL IT, YOU FILL IT"!

YOU'LL BE SURPRISED AT THE POWER THAT "**CALLING**" SOMETHING CAN STILL HAVE!

SHOTGUN!

I GOT THAT LAST SLICE OF PEPPERONI!

IF YOU'RE AN ADULT, BUT IMMATURE ENOUGH TO ADHERE TO THESE TYPES OF LAWS, YOU NEED THE ADVANTAGE OF PROFESSIONAL LEGAL ADVICE!

CHILDREN'S LAWS:

THEY'RE NOT JUST FOR CHILDREN ANYMORE!

by RUBEN BOLLING
TOMDBUG@AOL.COM

COMING SOON TO U.S.A. NETWORK: THE SHOW YOU FONDLY REMEMBER...

HOSPITAL 1973!

GOOD LORD. IT'S HIDEOUS.

POOR KID. IT'S WORSE THAN WE FEARED.

THIS BOY IS TOTALLY DEVOID OF **ANY SIDEBURNS** WHATSOEVER!

TO GO THROUGH LIFE LIKE THAT!

DOCTORS? THE BOY'S MOTHER IS WAITING.

I'LL TALK TO HER! RUN TESTS! LOTS OF THEM!

IS TIMMY ALRIGHT?! WHEN I SAW THAT HE ATE A HANDFUL OF "FLINT-STONES" VITAMINS, I RUSHED HIM RIGHT OVER!

THAT'S NOT TIMMY'S PROBLEM, MRS. PHILIPS.

BRACE YOURSELF-- TIMMY'S CHEEKS AND JAWLINE ARE **UTTERLY HAIRLESS!**

NOW, HE DOESN'T SEEM TO BE IN ANY PAIN, AND THERE **ARE** TREATMENTS, EXPERI-MENTAL IN NATURE...

DOCTOR, TIMMY'S A FOUR-YEAR-OLD **BOY**...

...SO I DON'T UNDERSTAND...

MRS. PHILIPS, IF I MAY INTER-RUPT, I DON'T WANT TO ALARM YOU, BUT...

..._YOU'VE_ GOT NO SIDEBURNS!

STRETCHER! STAT!

NEXT: SIDEBURN DEFICIENCY SYNDROME _EPIDEMIC!_

BY RUBEN BOLLING
TOMDBUG@AOL.COM

DIST. BY QUATERNARY FEATURES - ©1996 R. BOLLING

NEWS of the TIMES

U.S. ANNOUNCES PLAN TO "GO GAY"

UNDER RELENTLESS PRESSURE FROM THE **MEDIA ELITE**, THE FEDERAL GOVERNMENT ANNOUNCED THAT THE UNITED STATES WILL HENCEFORTH BE **GAY-IFIED**.

IT'S NOT JUST THAT ADORABLE "ELLEN" SHOW. JUST ABOUT EVERY T.V. PROGRAM HAS A POSITIVELY-PORTRAYED "**GAY FRIEND**" CHARACTER IN IT.

WE'RE LEFT WITH NO CHOICE.

LEGAL EXPERT GENE MEDINA EXPLAINS THAT GAYNESS WILL BECOME THE OFFICIAL SEXUALITY OF THE COUNTRY.

HETEROSEXUALITY WILL BE LEGAL BUT DISCOURAGED.

NO, WAIT... ILLEGAL BUT NOT PROSECUTED.

...USUALLY.

THERE ARE SOME DISSENTING VOICES. CONSERVATIVE POLITICAL CONSULTANT WILLIAM DOUGHERTY:

I THINK AMERICANS SHOULD REJECT THIS MOVE TOWARD THIS DEPRAVED AND IMMORAL LIFESTYLE.

AND MY ROOMMATE AGREES.

SPOKESGAYPERSONS HAVE BEEN UNMOVED BY PREDICTIONS OF THE DISASTROUS LONG-TERM EFFECTS THE PLAN COULD HAVE ON U.S. POPULATION.

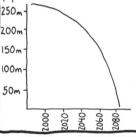

pop.
250m
200m
150m
100m
50m

2000 2020 2040 2060 2080

SUSAN WOLTREN, A T.V. PRODUCER AND NOTED GAY PERSON:

WE'RE GLAD EVERYONE IS GOING GAY NOW, AND WE DON'T CARE ABOUT THE CONSEQUENCES. IT'S BEEN OUR PLAN ALL ALONG.

CITIZENS ARE BEING ADVISED OF THE CORRECT WAY TO "GO GAY" IN A PUBLIC EDUCATION CAMPAIGN.

DOUG SEZ: Remember not to say, "I've become gay" but rather "I've realized I <u>am</u> gay." It adds credibility.

Go Gay. It's the Law.

MOST AMERICANS ARE ACCEPTING THE CHALLENGE, ALTHOUGH ON THEIR OWN TERMS.

I WILL BECOME GAY, BUT ONLY THE CLOSETED, REPRESSED KIND SO THAT I MAY CONTINUE TO MAKE LOVE TO MY LOVELY WIFE RITA EVERY SATURDAY NIGHT.

"NINA" APPEARS IN THE WEEKLY COMIC STRIP "NINA'S ADVENTURES" BY NINA PALEY

Nina
-MEETS-
Charley
THE AUSTRALOPITHECINE*

* AN APE-LIKE ANCESTOR OF HUMANITY FROM THE PLIOCENE EPOCH.

UM... MIND IF I JOIN YOU...?

SURE, AS IF THE GUYS I MEET AREN'T PRIMITIVE ENOUGH-- NOW IT'S AN ACTUAL APE-MAN!

HEY, I RESENT THAT! I MAY BE PRIMITIVE, BUT I'M NO MACHO CHAUVINIST! SEXISM IS A MODERN PHENOMENON!

YOUR MISCONCEPTION STARTED WHEN MALE-CENTRIC ANTHROPOLOGISTS OF THE EARLY 60'S BASED THEIR MODELS OF EARLY HOMINID SOCIETIES ON EXTANT BABOON TROOPS, WHICH CONSIST OF MALE-DOMINATED HAREMS!

THE CURRENT THINKING IS THAT AUSTRALOPITHECINE SOCIETIES WERE MORE LIKE CHIMPANZEE GROUPS ARE -- EGALITARIAN!!

BOTH SEXES COOPERATED IN CHILD-REARING AND RE-SOURCE GATHERING, AND AUS-TRALOPITHECINE MALES TREATED FEMALES WITH FULL RESPECT AS EQUALS!

WOW! TELL ME MORE!

WE ALSO KNOW WHAT TO SAY TO THE CHICKS!

DIST. BY QUATERNARY FEATURES · P.O. BOX 72 · NY · NY · 10021 · © 1994 RUBEN BOLLING ~ EMAIL: TOMDBUG@AOL.COM

ELECTRONIC MAIL: TOMDBUG @ AOL.COM

DIST. BY QUATERNARY FEATURES · P.O. BOX 72 · N.Y. · N.Y. · 10021

the "TOM THE DANCING BUG" COMIC STRIP Presents...

WRITTEN AND ILLUSTRATED BY your PAL RUBEN BOLLING

THE SECRET SHAME of TERRENCE

SECOND IN A SERIES OF INSTRUCTIONAL AND MOTIVATIONAL PICTURE STORIES PROMOTING PROPER USAGE OF REMOTE CONTROL DEVICES

SAY, TERRENCE, MAY I HAVE A WORD WITH YOU?

OH, YOU WANT SOME MORE OF JOAN'S FAMOUS SPONGE CAKE?

HA HA! YES, CATHERINE AND I HAD A WONDERFUL TIME AT YOUR PLACE LAST NIGHT, BUT...WELL, THIS IS DIFFICULT TO SAY...

PLEASE, CHAD! WHAT IS IT?!

I COULDN'T HELP NOTICING WHEN WE WATCHED TELEVISION AFTER DINNER, JOAN HANDLED THE REMOTE CONTROL!!

TERRENCE, YOU CAN'T LET A WOMAN HANDLE THE REMOTE! IT'S JUST NOT RIGHT!!

I KNOW! I FEEL SO... WEAK WHEN SHE DOES THAT, ESPECIALLY IN FRONT OF FRIENDS! BUT WHAT CAN I DO?!

YOU'VE GOT TO PUT THIS ISSUE TO HER FORCEFULLY, TERRENCE--

BE A MAN!!

NEXT DAY: SO, TERRENCE, ARE THINGS MORE NORMAL IN YOUR HOME NOW?

NO PROBLEM, CHAD!

SHE JUST SAID, "WHAT'S THE BIG DEAL? GO AHEAD--HOLD THE REMOTE."

HA HA! SILLY WOMEN! THEY JUST DON'T GET IT!!

End

DIST. BY QUATERNARY FEATURES, P.O. BOX 72, NY-NY-10021 · ©1995 R. BOLLING · EMAIL: TOMBUG@AOL.COM

May 16. In the middle of N.Y.P.D. Blue, cable goes out. There is Bad Reseption where I live, so I go to bed early.

May 17. Cable still out. Woke up better rested than usual. Great day at work, then met a friend and then brought home some magazines.

May 18. Cable still out. I feel great, though. I went jogging after work and then went to the library to get some books. Began reading.

May 19. After dinner with some friends I hadn't seen in a while, I finished reading East of Eden. I spent the rest of the evening contemplating humanity's inherent nature. Cable still out.

May 20. I began volunteering at a homeless shelter. I met another volunteer there, Jill, who seems very nice. Cable still out.

May 21. I'm sending out resumes in an attempt to escape my current dreary employment. I finished Chapter 3 of the novel I've started writing, and my first date with Jill was delightful. Cable still out.

May 22. I feel as though a fog has been lifted and I'm living for the first time! I never realized that television was such an insidiously stifling presence.

DEMON BOX! THIEF OF TIME! I FORSAKE YOU!

FAREWELL FOREVER, PURVEYOR OF INANITY!

FZZZ.

...I'd like to buy a vowel, Pat.

May 23. Big day! On Home Improovment, Al almost took a job in another city, but then he didn't.

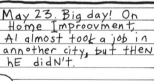

BY RUBEN BOLLING
TOMDBUG@AOL.COM

DIST. BY QUATERNARY FEATURES ·©1996 R. BOLLING

HI, KARYN. WHAT A DAY, HUH?

UHH! ENDLESS!!

AND I KEEP THINKING TODAY IS **THURSDAY!**

UHH! I KNOW! AND IT'S ONLY **TUESDAY!**

YOU KNOW WHY? BECAUSE **YESTERDAY** FELT LIKE A **WEDNESDAY!**

YEAH! ISN'T THAT WEIRD?

NEAL, DOESN'T TODAY FEEL LIKE A THURSDAY?

HUH? THURSDAYS DON'T **HAVE** A "FEEL"!

WHAT?!

ONLY MONDAYS, FRIDAYS, SATURDAYS AND SUNDAYS HAVE "FEELS."

OH, COME ON!

THERE'S NO DIFFERENCE BETWEEN THE **FEEL** OF A **THURSDAY** AND **TUESDAY!**

IT'S IN THE **NEWSPAPER**, SMART GUY!

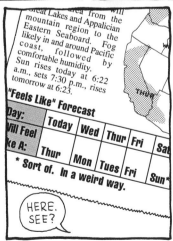

Great Lakes area from the mountain region to the Eastern Seaboard. Fog likely in and around Pacific coast, followed by comfortable humidity. Sun rises today at 6:22 a.m., sets 7:30 p.m., rises tomorrow at 6:23.

THUR

"Feels Like" Forecast

Day: Will Feel Like A:	Today	Wed	Thur	Fri	Sat
	Thur	Mon	Tues	Fri	Sun*

* Sort of. In a weird way.

HERE. SEE?

HMM... I GUESS THAT'S WHY I KEPT THINKING "SEINFELD" WOULD BE ON TONIGHT.

UHH! TOMORROW'S GOING TO FEEL LIKE A **MONDAY?!** I'M CALLING IN SICK!

UHH!

by Ruben Bolling

DIST. BY QUATERNARY FEATURES

GOD'S REELECTION CAMPAIGN

"MY 12 BILLION-YEAR TERM IS ALMOST UP.. AND I NEED *YOUR* SUPPORT FOR 12 BILLION MORE!!"

GOD for SUPREME DEITY

"Hey, His *name* is God!"

THE CAMPAIGN WAS NOT GOING WELL. GOD'S PREVIOUS INACCESSIBILITY MADE HIS ATTEMPTS AT POSITIVE PUBLICITY SEEM DISINGENUOUS.

...AND I'M SURE THIS NEW SHOPPING MALL WILL BRING PROSPERITY TO THE WHOLE TRI-COUNTY AREA..

HEY, GOD! I PRAYED FOR A JOB EIGHT MONTHS AGO, AND I'M STILL OUT OF WORK!

EMBOLDENED BY THE POSSIBILITY OF AN OUSTER, PEOPLE BEGAN EXPRESSING THEIR DISSATISFACTION.

FACES IN THE CROWD.

Dirk Valle Construction Worker "Famine, disease, misery, disasters.. I say throw the Bum out."

Sally Reemer Legal Secretar... "What's H... ever

GOD'S OPPONENT, NORM DRUCKER, A SUCCESSFUL ENTREPENEUR, RAN ON A BUSINESS APPROACH.

I RUN A PRETTY DARN GOOD CHAIN OF CAR DEALERSHIPS. I THINK I CAN RUN THE UNIVERSE *EVEN BETTER!*

DRUCK...

DRUCKER'S LITANY OF PROPOSALS WERE REAL CROWD PLEASERS.

NORM DRUCKER ☆FOR☆ SUPREME DEITY

JUST A FEW MORE *NEW IDEAS* FROM NORM DRUCKER:

#134 A NEW BEVERAGE-HOLDING APPENDAGE ON ALL HUMANS
#135 WAFFLE TREES
#136 NO GRAVITY ONE HOUR EACH DAY
#137 TALKING LLAMAS

GOD TRIED TO COUNTER BY REVOKING SOME OF HIS LESS POPULAR TENETS, BUT THE POLLS WOULDN'T BUDGE.

OKAY. YOU CAN USE MY NAME IN VAIN. AND I'M LOOKING INTO THE ADULTERY THING...

LIVE

IN A FINAL DEBATE, GOD'S DIVINE WISDOM WAS NO MATCH FOR DRUCKER'S SENSATIONAL PROMISES.

HE DOESN'T KNOW ANYTHING ABOUT RULING THE COSMOS! EVIL IS **NECESSARY** IN ORDER FOR GOOD TO **EXIST**!!

EVIL! GONE! FIRST 100 DAYS!

BUT IN THE END, GOD SHOWED WHY AN OMNIPOTENT INCUMBENT IS SO TOUGH TO BEAT.

NEW YORK BUGLE

GOD WINS IN "MIRACULOUS" UPSET!

Drucker Suddenly Afflicted With Boils